Praise for T

"Back in high school Hansen told my brother Chris he was hilarious. The rest of us may need a bit more direction in finding our own bliss—this book is it!"

~Tom Farley, *The Chris Farley Show*
NY Times and *LA Times* bestseller

"JP Hansen's book *The Bliss List* helps the reader navigate the world of work and find career opportunities that will ignite their passions and make going to work an exciting adventure."

—Chris Policinski,
CEO of Land O'Lakes

"*The Bliss List* is more than a book about careers. It is a practical guide and an enjoyable read, where Hansen takes you down the path to real happiness in your work and life."

—Shoya Zichy, *Career Match: Connecting Who You Are With What You'll Love To Do* and *Women And The Leadership Q: Revealing the Four Paths to Influence and Power*

"People come up to me all the time and say 'I always wanted to write a book' or 'I always wanted to do a radio talk show' and I always ask them the same question... 'Why don't you?'

"Too many people limit themselves from what they really want out of life. They put up obstacles that prevent them from being who they really want to be. They talk themselves out of getting that dream job.

"*The Bliss List* helps motivate, inspire, and train people to follow their dreams.

"Some people say that life is too short. Personally I believe that life is too long for you not to be following your own individual bliss."

—Tom Becka, *There's No Business Without the Show! Using Showbiz Skills to Get Blockbuster Sales!*

BE YOUR BLISS!

THE B1iss L1st

THE ULTIMATE GUIDE TO LIVING THE DREAM AT WORK AND **BEYOND!**

Re John Bliss.

J.P. HANSEN

Executive Recruiter • Helping millions of people find their bliss

THE B1iss L ST

THE ULTIMATE GUIDE TO LIVING THE DREAM AT WORK AND *BEYOND!*

CAREER BLISS PUBLICATIONS
OMAHA, NE

ISBN10: 0-9840934-1-9
ISBN13: 978-0-9840934-1-0
Library of Congress Control Number: 2009930144

Publisher Cataloging in Publication Data

Hansen, J. P. (James Parker)
The bliss list : the ultimate guide to living the dream and beyond / J. P. Hansen. – 1st ed.

xii, p. ; cm. *
Includes index and acknowledgments.
ISBN 978-0-9840934-1-0 (pbk.)
ISBN 0-9840934-1-9 (pbk.)

1. Job hunting.   2. Career changes.   3. Career development.

HF5382.7.H36 2009
650.14 – dc22   2009930144

Different preference for subject category would change the number:
Job hunting – HF5382.7
Career changes – HF5384
Career development, vocational guidance -- HF5381

Career Bliss Publications, Inc.
13518 L St.
Omaha, Nebraska 68137
www.YourBlissList.com

Book Design: Gary James Withrow
Production, Distribution, and Marketing: Concierge Marketing Inc.

Printed in the United States of America

10 9 8 7 6 5 4 3 2 1

This book is dedicated to the loving memory of my mother, Mary C. Hansen.

Contents

Introduction:
The Secret
of Success

> *"The secret of success is to make your vocation your vacation."*
> Mark Twain

id you pick up this book because you are unhappy in your current job? Do you want more from your work and from life? You are not alone. We all want bliss in our lives! America is in the midst of a crisis—a workplace crisis.

According to recent statistics, and backed up by my own experience over fifteen years as a successful executive recruiter: Four out of five people are unhappy in their current jobs!

That's 80 percent! Why is this?

Part of the answer is what we can learn from that fifth person who is "happy" in his or her current job. If you are part of the 80 percent who are unhappy, this book will definitely help you; if you are part of the 20 percent who are happy, this book will help you in unexpected ways, either by enhancing your current job or leading you to a new one.

The Bliss List will help you discover your bliss, then get you into your bliss zone, then harness it, and, finally, make your bliss actionable—for your vocation (and life).

What could cause an unhappiness rate of 80 percent?

For the past twenty-five years, corporate America has been through a significant number of downsizings, mergers and acquisitions (another phrase for downsizing,) and bankruptcies. Every time a consultant is hired by a company, the so-called advice inevitably results in layoffs. I have worked for four companies prior to starting my own company. Every single company for whom I worked either sold outright or divested the entire division that I was in.

I know I'm not alone. For the last fifteen years, I have owned an executive search business, and it often seems as if it is an "outplacement center," given all of the people I speak with just after being downsized (a nicer way to say, "You're fired!"). It is hard to find attitudinal bliss in a workforce in which you are living with a constant threat of being canned.

On a somewhat deeper level, one of the main causes of unhappiness is society. Think about it. Let's say you will live to the age of eighty. Where do you spend most of your time? If you said "sleeping," give yourself a pat on the back or, better yet, a nap. What is a close second? Working.

Sleeping and working: this is really your life. Take out two weeks for a vacation and you are spending 2,000 hours in any given year working. This assumes you *only* work forty hours per week. Add seven hours of sleep per night, and sleeping and working represent close to two-thirds of your time. Not much time is left for anything else.

The Bliss List will primarily focus on the number-one occupier of your waking time—your job. But the lessons you will learn will carry over into all facets of your life.

What does unhappiness in your job have to do with society?

You spent the first eighteen or so years of your life with little or no work stress. Your parents took care of you—providing clothing, food, and shelter, and paying the tab for almost everything else. You slept even more than seven hours per day during childhood and could sleep all day during the teenage years (and on some days you did). Work or work stress didn't enter the equation.

Then you reached the cut-off point—the last year of school, whether it was high school, college, or graduate school. This is the "uh oh, what do I do now?" phase. And it's quick—too quick for most.

Your conditioning up to this point had been sleep, play, and study—with very little work.

Unless you are independently wealthy, you will work at least 86,000 hours in your lifetime (starting at age twenty-two and retiring at age sixty-five). Yet, the time spent deciding what to do is miniscule. As graduation approached, you panicked, thinking what am I going to do? You had a lot of years to prepare, but probably didn't.

Now, with the real world looming, the pressure on finding a job built. Your parents, who had been footing your bill, may have even mentioned the importance of finding a job. Thus, your first job was usually decided on a whim—*I'll go with whoever offers me the most money,* or *I'll take the first job I can get.*

This is not exactly the most solid ground on which to make a great decision, let alone lead you to an ideal job. With new pressure, it left almost no time to truly decide which job would be right. Given the 86,000 working hours that await you, is it any surprise that, at age twenty-two, you didn't find that ideal job?

Are you one of these people? Be honest now. If you qualify, go easy on yourself. You are definitely not alone. But there is help.

A disciplined mind succeeds and an undisciplined mind fails. *The Bliss List* will help you develop a disciplined mind at whatever stage of life and work you are in.

This book will teach you to stop living your life in default and to take control of your job (and life)—starting today. You can make things happen for yourself.

Why isn't there a course on seeking and finding your blissful dream job during your formal education phase? On average, you spend eighteen years sitting in school without gaining much practical knowledge for the real world. It's no surprise, then, that a whopping 80 percent of us are unhappy once we hit the real world.

I know I didn't learn many useful job-seeking skills in school, but I feel I have attained a couple of advanced degrees in the amount of information that I have devoured over the last thirty years. I have read hundreds of books, listened to hours and hours of CDs and tapes, and watched hours on end of DVDs/videos on mystical insights from many enlightened people throughout time. Add these to hundreds of books on business acumen from some impressive business geniuses.

Yet I have never read a book that put it all together for me. If you are going to spend an average of 86,000 hours working, there should be an all-in-one book to help you find bliss—in your work and life. This book will help you discover your work—the passionate point when time stands still for you, and then you will receive practical advice on how to obtain it.

Defining Bliss

Dr. Martin Luther King, Jr., said, "Take the first step in faith. You don't have to see the whole staircase. Just take the first step." Reading this book is the first important step toward reaching what so many of you are missing in life: bliss! Simply defined, *bliss* is happiness and meaning. My goal is to share insights with you. Some may seem controversial; some may rock your world. But after reading *The Bliss List*, you will grow personally and professionally. I guarantee it!

Congratulations on taking the first step. My promise is that after reading this book you will find bliss in life and land that elusive dream job. It may even be more than one vocation. I have worked for over thirty-one years in a wide variety of jobs. I am fortunate to have worked in several dream jobs in my lifetime (so far). As an executive recruiter, I have helped thousands of people find their bliss through their work for over fifteen years (and with this book I hope to reach millions and help them find their bliss).

You are always growing and obtaining new peaks (and experiencing some valleys). This book will help you reach new peaks that may have seemed unreachable before. And then to reach new ones. There will be no room for valleys from here on.

We are spiritual beings living in a physical presence. *The Bliss List* will combine the practical with the mystical. The advice you gain from this book—obtaining true joy from your work—will also help you transform your life in every area.

I have been blessed with good fortune throughout my career and life. My dreams have been realized many times. I graduated from Boston College, my first choice, and then obtained several dream jobs with blue-chip companies like Nestle, Bristol-Myers Squibb, SC Johnson Wax, and ConAgra. I worked with some very talented people and was lucky to have several mentors who "taught me the ropes," and who continue to help me.

I became a self-made millionaire by age thirty-seven. After being the youngest Vice President (at age thirty-one) with a Fortune 35 company, I am now the President of a highly successful executive search company and have helped thousands of job seekers find true bliss. I owned a gorgeous dream house outright. That's right, with no mortgage. I owned a prime villa on beautiful Hilton Head Island outright. I owned a BMW outright.

The feeling of financial freedom was incredible, but it has not always been easy street for me. I have had my down years—my own valleys. And when I did, I bounced back. My experiences—good and bad—are real and captured in this book, so my book offers real-life, practical insight that will help you.

Applying Dr. Martin Luther King, Jr.'s belief that things happen in steps, the same was true for me in landing my ultimate dream job: owning my own business. Before I could obtain it, though, I knew I needed more training (and credibility). I have interviewed for several jobs and been the interviewer, plus I serve as a career coach in my role as an executive recruiter.

Along the way, I was able to obtain seven different dream jobs and some *not exactlys,* which ultimately gave me the experience and courage that I needed to start my own company.

If you view your own bliss as a series of steps, you will constantly be in a dream job state, regardless of your occupation. You will always be living in ultimate bliss.

Though my career may seem like a cake walk, don't think it was easy. Every single company and/or division for which I worked was sold within the first year of my employment. Many people with whom I worked were pulled under by a wave of negativity. Nevertheless, I never allowed myself to sway from my belief that I would one day have my own business and live with abundant financial prosperity.

Many Quantum Physicists believe that there are at least eleven parallel universes. That means that there is a place already where you are a multi-millionaire, living in a dream life with a dream job (you just have to find the keys to unlock that door). That's what we're working on.

Tell Me about Yourself

*"Follow your bliss and doors will open
where there were no doors before."*
Joseph Campbell

One of the many things I enjoy about being an executive recruiter is that I get to wear several hats in my job. One of those hats is psychologist. People pour out their hearts and share their inner secrets with me all the time. I have developed the skill of quickly determining whether someone is appropriate for a given job search I'm conducting.

I follow a simple but effective method: I start by giving a brief thumbnail sketch of my background in order to build credibility and gain the person's trust. This only takes a minute or two, but is very powerful. Trust is the key to a strong relationship. After I feel I've built enough trust, I ask for a brief synopsis of the person's background. I then shut up (not a natural thing for me) and listen—very intently.

I learn a great deal after asking the question, "Tell me about yourself?" What the person answers reveals all that is important, how he or she feels about his or her background—a great barometer for future success (or failure in some cases). His or her energy level, how well he or she verbalizes thoughts, and his or her basic interview skills—if you can't eloquently tell me about yourself, how can you ever do well in an interview?

After hearing the person's answer in describing his or her background, I always say, "Wow, you have a terrific background. What do you want to do next?" You would be amazed at how many people stumble at this basic question. If I had a dollar for every time a person replied, "I'm not sure … what have you got?" I would no longer need to work. Isn't this the essence of what is keeping a person from achieving bliss?

If you don't know what you want to do, how can you have a blissful dream job? Sometimes, the answer is, "Well, I know it isn't what I'm doing now!" This is actually an important step in obtaining bliss—by using contrast. Sometimes, you need to state what you don't want in order to decide what you do want. Using our previous examples of happiness and unhappiness, we can see that sometimes this contrast is needed to developing our true goals.

I'll tell you the story of Gary.

I bought a dream house not too long ago. Here, the word *dream* really works because it was in foreclosure and in need of some drastic repairs and major remodeling. Many people looked at the house and passed on it (they thought I was dreaming to think I could fix it up). As a result, my ultimate dream house was on the market for over a year. The house had so much potential, and I could visualize what it would look like with some creative improvements.

Gary worked for the general contractor I hired for this remodeling job. He used to run his own remodeling business but fell on hard times and a nasty client or two and decided to have more security, so he went to work for someone else. Gary was very competent. He had a can-do attitude. No matter what I asked—and some of my requests/ideas were out there—Gary would always say with a prideful smile, "I can do that!" And he was right.

Despite this outward optimism, Gary had an inner roadblock: he was not happy in life. One day, Gary asked me if I could help him find a job. Using my method, I asked him what he wanted to do next? He shot back, "Well, I don't want to be a carpenter!"

I paused, and then asked again, "What do you want to do?"

Gary retorted, "I don't want to be a carpenter."

Looking somewhat annoyed, I asked a third time, "What is it you *want* to do?"

Gary's third answer was the same, "I *don't* want to be a carpenter."

It was almost like the biblical story of the apostle Peter denying knowing Jesus three times before the cock crows. Gary was denying himself three times. I waited for a moment and didn't hear any cock crowing, but began asking Gary some different questions.

After a short while, he determined that he really wanted to be in business for himself again. And that he was passionate about carpentry, but wanted to be able to do a wider range of work. He wanted to be a general contractor who was capable of doing any project himself.

It was easy for me to encourage him after seeing all the outstanding things he had done in my remodeling project. I asked him what was holding him back.

He responded, "My wife would leave me if I did."

I asked, "Why?"

His excuse was "the money." I took out a sheet of paper and did some basic math, applying the economics of business ownership. The result was a no-brainer. On paper, he saw he would conservatively double his income in his own business. He was running out of excuses.

We spent about a half hour dispelling all of his excuses—limitations, roadblocks, and mind pollution—which were keeping him from obtaining his blissful dream job. They were rooted in fear—fear of failure.

Over the next month, Gary began focusing on starting (re-starting) his own business. He would ask me my opinion about ideas, but rather than give him my take, I would try to draw the answer out of him. He was really focused on starting his own company. I could sense his enthusiasm. His vision for his own dream job was developed through contrast. Saying what he didn't want to do had opened him up to what he really wanted—his passion.

It was only a matter of time before Gary was ready to take action. He had set his goal and was very enthusiastic, but still lacked confidence. I knew he needed to take action. Action drives results, and results build confidence.

I told him to print up some company cards and make lawn signs. For a small amount of money and time invested, he could see if he could drum up some business and prove to his skeptical wife that the money would be greater. He developed a company name, registered it as a corporation, and began focusing on his dream job.

In just a matter of weeks, he obtained a couple of lucrative contracts and voilà—he was on his own. He was so enthusiastic, I could feel it. He was a changed man. And it really was simple: he shifted his thoughts from what he didn't want (with fear and doubt) and turned to what he really did want (with enthusiasm and confidence), and his dream job became reality. His wife is even happy. Doubling his income over his first two months didn't hurt.

Gary is living the dream and loves his work. Gary found his bliss. Now let's help you find yours.

1

Find Your Bliss

*"Nothing is more important
than reconnecting with your bliss.
Nothing is as rich.
Nothing is more real."*
Deepak Chopra

*Y*ou already possess your inner bliss—your dream job. And you will likely have more than one. For you to find your blissful dream job, you have to firmly believe this. By reading this book right now, you are moving one important step closer to obtaining your dream job, and finding bliss in your life. Your bliss is literally right around the corner.

Actually, your bliss is inside of you. My goal is to help you truly look inside yourself in order to discover what inspires you. You'll also examine external factors that may have blocked you from your own inner wisdom and eliminate them.

The first step in attracting your ideal job is to determine what makes your vocation feel like a vacation—what makes time stand still for you. The next step is to stay in your zone—your bliss zone.

Your *Bliss List*

It's time to do some honest soul searching, so let's take an assessment. You will assess your skills, your desires, and your goals. This is a vital step toward obtaining your bliss, whether at work or in your life.

Think of *The Bliss List* as your working diary—your personal guide to living the dream at work (and life). Keep notes with this book for easy reference.

For this important exercise, simply write down what makes you feel the happiest. It doesn't have to be work-related. What makes time stand still for you? This is your *Bliss List*. Is it living like a millionaire? Being your own boss? The security of a stable company? Skimming over a lake in a sailboat? Skiing down a mountain? Hiking in the wilderness? Reading a spellbinding book? You decide.

This list should come naturally to you and not take more than a few minutes for you to write. You actually will feel your mood improve as you think about, and write, this list. Whatever you write, the only rule is that you tell yourself what makes you happy—not what makes your spouse, family, boss, friends, clergy, or whoever happy. Don't place any limits on yourself.

I'll give you an amazing example of another person's list after you're done, but I don't want to sway you with it yet. This list needs to be your *Bliss List*. Write at least fifteen words and phrases now.

As promised, here's an example: Jack Canfield, world-renowned author of the bestselling Chicken Soup for the Soul series (over 110 million copies in print), compiled his passion points in *The Passion Test* by Janet Attwood and Chris Attwood. This was his *Bliss List*:

1. Being of service to massive numbers of people

2. Having an international impact

3. Enjoying celebrity status

4. Being part of a dynamic team

5. Having a leadership role

6. Helping people live their vision

7. Speaking to large groups

8. Having an impact through television

9. Being a multimillionaire

10. Having world-class headquarters and support team

11. Having lots of free time

12. Studying with spiritual masters regularly

13. Being part of a spiritual leader's network

14. Creating a core group of ongoing trainers who feel identified with my organization

15. Having fun, fun, fun!

I use Jack Canfield's list for a reason. Jack is an enormously successful man who has had a positive influence on the entire world. And his list reflects that. I especially liked his number one: "Being of service to massive numbers of people." Wow!

The bestselling author Jose Silva wrote that if you could help two additional people in anything you desire, you greatly increase your chances of manifesting it. I think being of service to massive numbers of people qualifies—and Jack has done it. And continues to do it.

Does your list have a degree of challenge in it? Jack's certainly does. I'm not saying you must have Jack's list, but remember, your list has no boundaries or limits (neither did Jack's). The higher you set your goals, the greater your results. Don't short yourself on your *Bliss List*; challenge yourself. If you need to return to your *Bliss List* to add or modify any items, please do so before you continue reading.

Now, that you have completed your top fifteen, we'll cut it down to a top seven.

It has been scientifically proven that the human brain is capable of handling only seven things at once. To pare your list, simply compare and rank your 1 vs. 2, and then 1 vs. 3, then 1 vs. 4, and so on down the list. Whatever comes out on top at the end will make up your *Top Seven Bliss List*. These will now comprise your primary goals.

Post this list in plain sight (more on this later) and put one in your wallet or purse too. This list is you. The more concentrated thought you place against this list with enthusiastic feeling and confidence, the quicker all seven will manifest in your life. I want you to go seven for seven here.

Next, we're going to apply your *Top Seven* into a first draft for your ideal job. You may have more than one ideal job—the more, the better (no limits, remember?). So, with no further ado, you will simply write the title or titles of your dream job or jobs. Even if the title is fictitious, it doesn't matter; this is your blissful dream job after all.

Now, write down a brief description of what this job entails. Intersperse your *Top Seven* into it—they should be a match. Don't limit yourself to only salary. Think of what really makes you happy. The money will follow. What are you passionate about? Again, don't fret if it seems fictitious. The more you think of your dream jobs with enthusiasm and confidence, the more quickly fiction will turn into reality.

Next, write down what skills are necessary to do this job. Under this, write the skills you already possess. How does it match up? It probably is not too far off.

Write down what steps are needed. If more education is required, list it. Will you need additional education/credentials like a certification? Would a degree or an additional class or a training seminar or merely a different company environment help you to obtain what is missing? Be as honest as possible and take no shortcuts. This is your dream job.

We'll use an actual example of a client of mine. We'll call her Myra. The following is Myra's *Bliss List* and her dream job title and description, the necessary skills and how they match up, and steps needed to reach her dream job:

Myra's Bliss List

1. Being in a loving, passionate relationship with a man who sees the bigger picture in life.

2. Enjoying a close and loving relationship with my three children.

3. Living in a beautiful waterfront home on an island where I can go boating, paddle boarding, and kayaking.

4. Spending a three-month vacation on the Amalfi Coast of Italy and painting with a master.

5. Working as a Licensed Professional Counselor at a treatment center for girls (this center hasn't opened yet because it needs funding).

6. Having a leadership role as a therapist and as a teacher with families.

7. Giving people hope.

8. Being a part of a forward-thinking treatment team that believes in and implements positive psychotherapy.

9. Attending a weeklong workshop with a master of positive psychotherapy.

10. Having time for a great workout with weights and aerobics three times a week.

11. Owning a mountain house where I can ski in the winter.

12. Using my professional camera to capture the beauty of the world. Traveling with a famous photographer.

13. Walking my dogs on the beach every day.

14. Having a personal chef to cook healthy meals for me and for dinner parties with my friends.

15. Completing my LPC (Licensed Professional Counselor) certification.

Myra's Bliss List Top Seven

1. Being in a loving, passionate relationship with a man who sees the bigger picture in life.

2. Enjoying a close and loving relationship with my three children.

3. Living in a beautiful waterfront home on an island where I can go boating, paddle boarding, and kayaking.

4. Working as a Licensed Professional Counselor at a treatment center for girls (this center hasn't opened yet because it needs funding). Also, I am currently working on my LPC.

5. Having a leadership role as a therapist and as a teacher with families. Giving people hope.

6. Having time for a great workout with weights and aerobics three times a week.

7. Owning a mountain house where I can ski in the winter.

Dream Job Title

Licensed Professional Therapist in a comprehensive treatment program that specializes in the personal empowerment, recovery resource development, evidenced-based treatment, support services, recovery, and advocacy for girls ages twelve through seventeen. This facility is on a beautiful piece of property where the girls will kayak and participate in an outdoor activity component.

Dream Job Description:

Conduct weekly twelve-step meetings and daily meditation and reflection.

Facilitate group therapy sessions on psycho-educational, interpersonal skills, depression, impulse control, sober fun, co-dependency, substance abuse, among others.

Travel to beautiful retreat locations to learn, reinforce, and renew the spirituality of therapy (building personal relationships with the master teachers in the field of psychology).

Conduct individual therapy.

Instruct education groups on adolescent health issues including fitness and nutrition.

Facilitate family therapy and communication with parents through seminars and education.

Conduct psychological testing and assessment.

Teach physical fitness, yoga, meditation, and nutrition education.

Teach life skills.

Facilitate organic gardening and culinary skills.

Teach photography and appreciation of nature and the beauty of the countryside.

Facilitate the expression of creativity and self expression through painting.

Skills needed to do this job

License in professional counseling in South Carolina

Specialization in family and group counseling

Comprehensive understanding of nutrition and fitness

Knowledge of yoga and meditation skills

Knowledge of the fundamentals of photography

Good teaching and communication skills

An understanding of gardening and culinary skills

Skills I already possess:

Teacher for thirteen years

Comfortable presenting information

Masters in Education Counseling

Own and shoot a professional camera

Two yoga certifications

Workout five times a week and understand the fundamentals of fitness

Eat healthy and have a good understanding of nutrition

Good interpersonal skills

Steps needed to obtain my dream job:

Finish course requirements for my LPC.

Complete an internship.

Pass the state licensure exam.

Complete seminars or workshops in family and group work.

Obtain additional class in adolescent issues, eating disorders, crises intervention, substance abuse, and others.

Have the funding to open and staff the facility.

Turn Your *Bliss List* into Reality with Bliss Cards

It's time to start amplifying your desires. Whether you believe in the Law of Attraction or think it's merely fantasy, I believe the more you think of something with enthusiasm and confidence, the more likely you are to manifest your goals in your life.

The Law of Attraction has been spotlighted with a bestselling book and DVD *The Secret*. After selling millions of copies and getting airplay on popular shows with Oprah Winfrey and Larry King, this book explaining the Law of Attraction is no "secret" anymore.

We live in a world where science and spirituality coexist and even complement each other. This hasn't always been the case. The Law of Attraction is rooted in spirituality, but elements have been proven scientifically through quantum physics.

In a nutshell, the Law of Attraction says that your thoughts (both conscious and unconscious) dictate the reality of your life, whether or not you're aware of it. Essentially, if you really want something and believe it's possible, you'll probably get it. Conversely, putting a lot of attention and thought into something you don't want means you'll probably get that too. Everything in your life can be explained by the Law of Attraction—good and bad.

For this practical application of the Law of Attraction, you simply need some 3- x 5-inch cards. These will be your Bliss Cards. Write your *Top Seven Bliss List* items on a card and keep it with you wherever you go: in your wallet/purse, pocket, dashboard of your car, on your refrigerator, and in your briefcase. The idea is to keep your list in a strategic place where you are most apt to be able to view it during the day. Look at it as often as you can. It is a very powerful tool in turning your *Bliss List* into reality.

After you have received one or more of the items on your *Bliss List,* simply make a new one and save your card in a folder labeled *"Bliss List* Successes."

Also, your *Bliss List* may change; you actually want it to change— and to grow. Remember, you are energy and are always moving. You will evolve, and so will your list. Update it every three months or as needed.

Your *Top Seven Bliss List* on a simple Bliss Card is a powerful way to start the results ball rolling. It has worked for me and for countless others. Well-known motivational speaker Bob Proctor (featured in *The Secret*) credits his enormous wealth to these cards. He carries one with his goals at all times.

I know you may be a little skeptical. What do you have to lose? The cost for a few of these cards is pocket change; the return may be immeasurable especially if it leads you to your bliss.

Put yourself in the right frame of mind

Ever hear this phrase, "having the right frame of reference"? Or better yet, "putting yourself in the right frame of mind"? These little phrases are profound and hold an important key to obtaining your bliss in work and life.

"Reference point," for our discussion, means simply, emotions. If you are in a bad mood, guess what? Your point of attraction is bad, bringing you undesirable things. Conversely, if you are in a good mood, you will attract good, desirable things. There are two primary emotions: love and fear. They are polar opposites, and every emotion is a derivative of love and fear.

Beyond these two basic emotions, the following is an expanded basic reference point scale in order of most desirable to least:

1. Love
2. Gratitude/Appreciation
3. Bliss
4. Happiness
5. Peace
6. Freedom
7. Knowledge
8. Empowerment
9. Positive Expectation/Belief
10. Optimism
11. Hopefulness
12. Contentment

****

13. Boredom
14. Pessimism

15. Frustration/Impatience

16. Irritation

17. Disappointment

18. Doubt

19. Worry

20. Blame

21. Discouragement

22. Anger

23. Revenge

24. Hatred/Rage

25. Jealousy/Envy

26. Insecurity/Guilt/Unworthiness

27. Fear/Grief/Depression/Despair/Powerlessness

You are capable of feeling every single one of these emotional reference points. I have felt them all at one time or another. You have too. This is your ability to experience the full spectrum of emotions in life. This is the paradoxical concept of contrast: sometimes it takes feeling depressed to appreciate feeling happiness.

With the Law of Attraction, your attraction point is your emotional reference point. Prayer works this way. If you pray from a negative point of reference (emotions on the list from 13 through 27), you will negate your prayer; from a positive reference point (using emotions from 1 through 12), you will be able to attract your desired prayer.

Ever pray? Ever meditate? Those of you who say you would never meditate, or don't believe in meditation, already meditate through prayer. Prayer is deep thought with feeling. See any metaphor for your blissful dream job? I hope so.

Your point of reference needs to be in the positive area (emotions 1 through 12) if you are going to attract your bliss. The trick is getting there. It's not as hard as you may think. You control your point of reference. That's right, you can consciously choose to be in a loving, peaceful state, or you can choose to be upset with seemingly everything around you.

Remember, your bliss lies within you already. All you need to do is unlock it, find it, and follow it. Be in a positive frame of mind at least 95 percent of the time, and the majority of your results will be positive.

Making Your *Bliss List* Work

The exercises you just completed were a very important step toward obtaining your blissful dream job. Just writing down your *Top Seven Bliss List* is powerful. It sets your goals in motion, and you will begin attracting what you intend with enthusiastic confidence every time.

Here are ways you can make your *Top Seven Bliss List* work for you with more force, increasing its intensity (raising your vibrations). Remember, set your goal with enthusiasm and confidence. Writing the *Bliss List* is the start of your goal-setting. Developing the right frame of mind to receive your goal is equally important. Do the following:

- Review your *Bliss List* at least three times a day.
- Ask yourself, "Am I choosing a path that will lead me toward my *Bliss List* or away from it?" every time you are faced with a decision.
- Keep your frame of mind (emotional state) positive at least 95 percent of the time. If you stray, catch yourself, say "Cancel," and think of something that makes you laugh.

- Meditate three times per day for fifteen minutes (or do some other quiet activity such as prayer that brings you peace of mind).
- Develop an attitude of gratitude.
- Follow a healthy lifestyle that includes exercise and healthful foods.
- Think of your *Bliss List* in the present tense—as if it has already happened.

The more you can imagine your *Bliss List* has already happened (with confidence), the more likely you are to obtain that dream job.

Now, let's strengthen the list with a simple but highly effective exercise. Write out five measures of success that will happen when you are in your blissful dream job. The following are some examples:

Bliss List: I am a famous author.

Measures of success—

1. I have been on *The New York Times*' bestseller list.
2. I have reached over 1 million readers worldwide.
3. I earn over $1 million each year on book sales.
4. I have been interviewed on popular TV and radio shows.
5. My books are carried in all major libraries and bookstores.

Bliss List: I am serving humanity.

Measures of success—

1. I have influenced millions of people.
2. I have received thousands of testimonials from people sharing how I have improved their lives.
3. I am making the world a better place to live each day.
4. My books are carried in all major libraries and bookstores.
5. My messages have been quoted by others who are serving humanity.

Bliss List: I own a dream house on the ocean.

Measures of success—

1. The view from my patio is spectacular.
2. I hear seagulls every morning.
3. I see the sunrise over the water each morning.
4. My house is valued at over $2 million.
5. I enjoy swimming in the ocean and walking along the shore each day.

Nine out of ten people say they are more productive when they are around positive people, according to the authors of *How Full Is Your Bucket?*

Create Your Bliss Board

The more intensity you give to your thoughts, the stronger they become. Your attention to your goals allows them to manifest more quickly in your life. A powerful tool to help you strengthen your thoughts and vibration—and to help you obtain your bliss more quickly—is to use a Bliss Board.

As the name implies, basically it is like a bulletin board. It is comprised of your goals and desires. Vivid, colorful pictures are ideal and very powerful. Fill your Bliss Board with the top phrases that describe what makes you happy. Whatever you desire and think about with enthusiasm and confidence will manifest itself.

You can have more than one Bliss Board. I keep at least three Bliss Boards in my office, along with framed affirmations such as these: "Money Comes Easily and Frequently," "Every Day, in Every Way, I am Getting Better, Better, and Better," "Negative Thoughts, Negative Suggestions, Have No Influence over Me at Any Level of Mind," and "Desire, Believe, Expect, and Be Grateful."

The trick is to keep your mind laser-focused on what you truly want. Meditating and visualizing your Bliss Boards and affirmations also magnifies your vibration tremendously. The more you can intensify your goals, the more likely you will obtain them.

Be creative with your Bliss Board. Have fun with it. The more realistic you can make it—using pictures in 3D and colors that appeal to you—the more effective it will be. Cut out pictures from magazines or print colored images from the Internet. Place your Bliss Board in a prominent location where you will see it often.

I keep my three Bliss Boards at eye level right around my computer screen, and every time I look at them (and it is often), I always try to feel as though my goals and desires are in the present—as if I already have them.

What is on my three Bliss Boards? My first is simply for "Harmonic Wealth: Financial, Relational, Intellectual, Physical, and Spiritual." My second Bliss Board pertains to this book: "#1 Bestseller, Help More Than 100,000 People, Financial Independence, Abundant Prosperity, and an appearance on a popular TV or radio talk show." My third is a copy of the cover page for this book. Since you are one of the 100,000 who bought this book and are actually reading it, I am one step closer to one of my goals. I am grateful for you.

Do a Bliss Board. It only takes a few minutes to do. You already have a *Top Seven Bliss List*, so it should be easy—and fun. The results will amaze you.

Fill Your Bliss Jar

Take a jar (I use an empty green-olive jar from my favorite brand) and tape a note on top of the jar stating, "Whatever is contained in this

Bliss Jar—IS!" Write each goal individually on a small piece of paper, then reread it with enthusiastic feeling, and simply drop each one into the jar. You will be amazed at how many of your little notes actually come true.

Now, write your blissful dream job and be as specific as you can and reread it; then drop it into your jar.

Every single goal I have deposited into my Bliss Jar has miraculously come true. Bliss Jars make miracles seem common. It takes only a few minutes, but the results will astound you (at first).

To get started, you may want to use the fifteen items you listed in your original *Bliss List*. Though you pared the list down to seven so you wouldn't overload your brain, capable of handling only seven things at once, you cannot overload your Bliss Jar. There are no limits. Write all fifteen goals down separately and drop 'em into the jar. It will start working its magic right after you close the lid on the jar.

The first time something you wrote comes true—and it will—start a new jar. Label it your "Gratitude Jar" and pop each item as it comes true into the new jar. This will serve as a constant reminder of your gratitude and the fact that your Bliss Jar works.

The more you can formalize your thoughts, the more likely your goals will manifest. Bliss Lists, Cards, Boards, and Jars all help bring your desires into reality.

In the next chapter, we will delve into pitfalls that can derail you from your bliss. As you improve your focus on what you truly want, while avoiding obstacles, you will find your bliss.

2

Four-Letter Words,
Buckets, and
Other Positive
Ways to Change
Your Attitude
and Your Mind

Change is eternal,
progress divine

From now on, four-letter words will no longer be allowed in your vocabulary. Four-letter words are seemingly everywhere: in our conversations, in books we read, in athletic events, in business circles, on radio, and certainly on TV. Four-letter words have become part of our psyche and are truly toxic.

You are probably thinking, "What's the big deal with saying or hearing *sh#t, f#%k* or *d&mn*?" I'm not referring to *those* words. Though those words, commonly referred to as *swear words,* are probably not the most enlightened form of communication, I'm referring to the most damaging of four-letter words: *can't, don't,* and *won't.*

The human spirit is truly limitless. Look at all the things that have been invented over the years by mankind: electricity, automobiles, airplanes, a space ship to the moon, and numerous cures for a host of diseases. In every case, one common denominator pervades: a positive attitude and a can-do approach.

Henry Ford, the inventor of the automobile, said, "Whether you think you can or think you can't, either way you are right." Profound.

At the time he was chasing his dream—a motorized form of transportation—people ridiculed him, calling him crazy for having such a wild vision. His friends actually tried to have him locked up in an insane asylum! Amid all the criticism from some very intelligent people, Henry Ford kept his dream alive with a positive attitude, always saying and believing *I think I can.*

Had he fallen into the trap of the four-letter words, do you think he would have invented anything, let alone something as complex as a motorized car? Absolutely not. Any time you say or think *can't, don't,* and *won't,* you are placing limits on yourself.

Think about it in terms of natural resources. Your greatest natural resource is yourself. Almost everyone at some point has experienced physical exhaustion through exercise. When you work out vigorously, you probably use 60 to 90 percent of your body's potential. You know this through the obvious sign of physical exhaustion—sweat. Sweat is your body's way of communicating that your physical movements in the form of exercise are working.

We work out to achieve desired goals: a better physique, losing weight, building muscle, for example. For the exercise to be successful, chances are you went into it with a positive attitude. I *can* run a mile in under eight minutes, I *can* lift one hundred pounds over my head, and I *can* ride my bike around the lake. After you achieve your goal, you feel good; if you fall short, you probably resolve to try harder next time and eventually achieve your goal. If a four-letter word enters your psyche though, you will never make it.

While I was coaching my son's fifth-grade basketball team, we put this theory to the test with free throws. We had just lost a close game (that we should have won) because we didn't make our free throws at the end of the game. The other team did. Since we practiced the shot more than any other team, I was puzzled. My instincts told me the problem wasn't physical (lack of practice) but attitudinal.

I pulled my team together and explained the power of a positive attitude and its direct proportion to success: in this case, making the shot. Conversely, I discussed what happens when negative thoughts enter your mind before shooting. The boys looked aloof and somewhat puzzled, giving me that "can't we just play, coach?" look. I knew I was running out of time with a bunch of ten-year-old boys, so we quickly put it to the test.

First, I had each boy mentally say, "Make the shot," and then shoot two free throws in a row; next, I had them shoot two more shots after mentally saying, "Don't miss." Remember, the subconscious mind doesn't discern between do and don't—it picks up the predominant thought—in this case, "miss."

The results were remarkable. The percentage of shots made with a positive thought versus a negative thought was over 50 percent. Those of you who understand basketball know that many games are decided by one point (a single free throw) and a 50 percent advantage was huge.

We further tested the theory with five shots and used the same positive and negative mantras. The results were even more compelling. The boys became believers in positive thinking, and we soon became the best free throw shooting team in the league. All it took was focusing their thoughts on a positive. Try this same exercise using any measuring stick. You don't need a basketball.

If you are like the average person, you will use less than 5 percent of your brain throughout your life. Drawing an analogy to our exercise example, you conversely use between 60 to 90 percent of your body while working out. Why the discrepancy? Is your physique that much more capable of working to its capacity than your mind?

You know the answer. Then why do you underutilize your mind? Do the four-letter words have anything to do with it? Of course, they do.

You place limits on yourself any time you say, "I can't do this" or "I won't try this" or "It doesn't work." Henry Ford figured it out: "Whether you think you can or think you can't, either way you are right." Your words reflect your thoughts and become your results.

If you are going to get your blissful dream job, you have to commit to dropping the four-letter words from your vocabulary, your thoughts, and your actions. These toxic terms infect your psyche and limit you to using less than 5 percent of your greatest natural resource—your mind. A positive can-do attitude is the difference between success and failure. It's that simple.

No Limits

You are created as an unlimited spiritual being. The only limitations you have are in your mind in the form of fear. What is fear? Fear is:

False

Evidence

Appearing

Real

If you hold the concept of limitation, it becomes reality, but the concept of limitation is not true. A hindrance (limitation) may appear real, but it is not. Four-letter words are a form of limitation. A toxic form. The great news is that all limitations can easily be released from you. They are *not you* to begin with.

You're probably saying, "Not me—I'd never let my mind become polluted!" I talk to people all the time who don't even realize they are doing it. I hear the following phrases/words often:

- *I'm not ever going to be rich.*
- *I'm not management material.*

- *I'm not smart enough.*
- *I'm fat because it's in my genes.*
- *I couldn't ever be like him/her.*
- *My father died at sixty-seven. I probably will too.*
  It's in my genes.
- *There's no way I could ever match that.*

Have you ever said any of these? They are all limitations. Are they real? Sure, if you make them real by placing your attention on any of them. The upshot: by using another universal law, the Law of Polarity, you can discharge all toxic limitations. They were not you to begin with, so they can be released with a little conscious effort using your disciplined mind.

The Law of Polarity states simply that everything has a polar opposite. For every positive, there is a negative (think of a magnet here): yin/yang, plus/minus, dark/light. Do you ever wonder why, in a world of unlimited abundance, you sometimes go through events, conditions, and circumstances that you perceive as unpleasant? Becoming aware and developing a deeper understanding concerning the Law of Polarity may provide the insight that you need to obtain your bliss:

- *Can't* becomes *can.*
- *Don't* becomes *do.*
- *Won't* becomes *will.*
- *I'm never going to be rich* becomes *money comes easily and frequently.*

The Story of Paul

I have known Paul for over twenty-five years. We were friends at Boston College, he was in my wedding party, and to this day, even though we live a thousand miles away, he has remained one of my closest friends.

Paul is very bright. He graduated as *Scholar of the College* at Boston College. While the rest of us were *partying like it was 1999* (in 1984), during our senior year, Paul was writing a one-hundred-plus-page mini-thesis, which later earned him his award.

After college, Paul attended Fordham Law School in New York near his hometown. He followed in his father's footsteps by attending law school. After excelling in law school, Paul passed the New York bar exam on his first try, and voilà, he was in his chosen profession. The only problem was that he hated it!

Paul changed firms a few times and even changed the types of law he practiced, but it didn't matter—he still hated it. Every time I would talk to him, he was in a state of depression—complaining about the money not being what he wanted, the high cost of having an office in Manhattan, and even the work itself. Paul was certainly among the four out of five people unhappy in their jobs.

For someone to attend graduate school for a chosen profession (especially the brutal three years of law school) and then hating it, the feeling of depression must have been devastating. It's a lot easier to quit that job flippin' burgers at McDonald's (my first job) than to walk away from a profession that was dearly earned and outwardly admired.

So, let's take a step back and examine Paul's dilemma. You might be thinking the same thing I was whenever I would visit with him: "You are a successful attorney, making good money, working in Manhattan, living in Westchester, married to a beautiful doctor, and having two gorgeous daughters. Paul, most people would trade places with you in an instant. What is the problem?"

The truth is all the externals didn't make his internal happy. He had zero passion for what he was doing. He was sinking in quicksand.

Rather than wallow in self-pity and ultimately self-destructing like so many others, Paul did something different. He changed his mindset and set some new goals. He developed a patent. He had an idea for a software enhancement, and he wrote it down. It was his "aha" moment. He felt tremendous joy because he knew it would be worth something someday.

Then, he did it again. He had another idea, and "BOOM," it turned into another patent. And then another. It was as if time stood still for Paul as he was doing this. His creative juices were flowing overtime, and he was rapidly becoming a patent expert.

While still going through the motions of being a lawyer, he used his spare time thinking about improving things in his daily life, and he wrote them down. He noticed the obvious: he was passionate about writing patents.

The next step was to see if his ideas had any value. He was blown away. His first patent was auctioned for six figures. The time it took him to have his idea was less than a minute and was now worth over $100,000. The second patent auction was also very lucrative. And so was the third. Paul was approached by a successful firm specializing in marketing patents and was asked to join them as a partner. He jumped at the offer.

Paul is like a new man—actually more like a little kid with a new toy. He is so upbeat, he's borderline giddy. Gone are his feelings of despair and depression. Long gone. In a short while, he has made a small fortune, but more importantly, he found his dream job. It doesn't feel like a job to him. He enjoys waking up and going to work. He is now part of a group that shares in the wealth of others' ideas.

While I was lounging with Paul poolside in Las Vegas, his cell phone rang. He found out he made another six figures—from someone else's efforts. Napoleon Hill (author of *Think and Grow Rich*) wrote about the power of joining forces with others with similar vision. Paul is now living proof of the wisdom of Napoleon Hill. On a personal note, Paul has lost weight, feels great, and is a man who is living the dream at work and beyond.

Let's take a minute to look at what happened to Paul. He became a lawyer with the strong influence of his father, who was a very successful attorney. Though Paul was successful in the profession of law, he was living someone else's dream—not his own. He gave it a shot, and when it wasn't what he wanted, he did the first thing needed to make a change. He attracted what he *did* want into his life. His ideas came to him with seemingly little effort. He set goals, had enthusiasm, and, as each idea materialized, his confidence grew.

A blissful dream job should feel like a *vacation,* not a *vocation.* Paul felt like he was on vacation. Time stood still for Paul. He followed his inner voice, his true passion, and it rewarded him. He knew he was meant to develop and market patents. To get there, though, Paul had the following:

- Vision. He focused his goals on what he wanted to do and the results followed.
- Belief. He believed in himself and in his ideas.
- Positive Attitude. While he was developing his ideas, he became optimistic.
- Awareness. He was tuned in to signs along the way and acted on them.
- Wisdom. He surprised even himself with his ideas.
- Initiative. He followed his inner push.
- Discipline. He made it a habit to create ideas.
- Action. He took the time to write down his ideas and apply them.
- Inner Success. Though the money was great, his real triumph was inner joy for finding what he was passionate about and doing it.

On the other hand, a number of obstacles like these could have gotten in his way derailing his dream job:

- *I don't have time* excuse. A toxic and limiting four-letter word. Less than a minute to make $100,000?
- *I can't do that* excuse. Four-letter word. He believed in himself.
- *I won't be able to sell this* excuse. Four-letter word. Defeatism.
- *My wife won't let me* excuse. Another four-letter word. Toxic.
- *My dad will think I'm nuts* excuse. In hindsight, your dad would think you were *nuts* for not doing this sooner. And if not, who cares. It's not his life or his dream job. Send him a copy of your bank statement, and he'll ask if he can join you.
- *I'll let my law partners down* excuse. Are they living your life? You are letting them down by being depressed about the very job you're trying to share with them. Misery never produced greatness unless it's expressed in a poem or a song.
- *My friends will think I'm crazy* excuse. Are they really your friends then? Your true friends want to see you happy first. If it means chasing your dream and they're not happy, well, it's definitely time for new friends. Mediocrity attacks excellence.

Get the picture? You may be saying, that's a great story, but I can't do that. Hopefully, by now, you will catch the four-letter word and reverse the toxic thought. I hope you said, "Hey! I could do that." And you could. And you will.

How many times have you seen something and said, "I could improve that?" It's what Paul did. It took him less than a minute for the idea to pop into his head. When it did, it felt right to him. He followed his sixth sense—his inner intuition. He acted on it and time stood still.

Now, I'm not saying your dream job needs to be Paul's, but it was easier for him to make that move than you think. And, aren't we all inventors? You see something that's broken and you fix it. No manuals needed; no graduate degree needed. You just do it. If you count the number of times you see something and think of a better way, you will amaze yourself. Paul acted on it. His confidence paid off.

First and foremost, Paul needed to develop a goal to break out of his doldrums, by saying, "I intend to find my bliss." Everyone can do that. Then, the more enthusiastically he desired it, the more his vision began manifesting itself. He was aware of signs along the way. He acted on those signs and persevered. His vocation became a vacation for him.

What is holding you back from obtaining your bliss? Everything is possible in your life.

Has anyone ever told you to do something because of money: "Be a doctor, you'll make lots of money"? Or in reverse, has anyone ever discouraged you with the threat of not making money: "There's not much money in that" or "Don't do that; you can't make any money doing that"? (Notice the four-letter words.) Did you ever receive advice like this? Did it sway you?

Plenty of doctors, lawyers, accountants, dentists, and executives earn good money but hate what they do. Paul is not the only example. How can this be? If money was their motivation, devoid of passion, are you surprised? There are many unhappy, wealthy people. I talk to them all day long in my executive search business.

External forces that cause you to stray from your inner wisdom need to be recognized and cancelled. Only your inner essence knows what is best for you.

Positive Psychology 101

Wouldn't this be a cool class to take in school? It isn't listed on any college curriculums yet, but if it were, I would sign up in a heartbeat.

What is the field of psychology based on? Hint: it's the opposite of positive. Picture the shrink, inviting you to lie down on his or her couch and, with a slight frown, asking, "What's wrong?"

By now, you've had a big enough dose of the Law of Attraction, so where does thinking about what's wrong fit in your frame of reference? What will focusing on what's wrong attract back to you? The answers: more of what's wrong. This form of psychology is wrong!

Imagine what would happen if psychology began focusing on *what's right* with people? Asking, "What's wrong with you?" automatically pops you into a negative reference point. It makes you feel lousy as you think of the answer and then even worsens as you begin to verbalize your response. Asking "What's right?" places you in a positive emotional state and makes you feel good as you formulate your answer to the question.

It only takes seventeen seconds to change your emotional mood. If you feel depressed, in merely seventeen seconds, by changing your thoughts to joy, gratitude, love, or happiness, you leave that depression behind and start attracting desirable results. Increasing your positive emotions could lengthen your lifespan by ten years.

In the 1950s, psychology professor Don Clifton, PhD, while teaching at the University of Nebraska, began researching and pioneering positive psychology. After conducting a significant number of interviews, Dr. Clifton wrote the fabulous book *How Full Is Your Bucket?* and later, as CEO of the Gallup Organization, began implementing positive psychology into one of the greatest corporate cultures in the world. In 2002, one year before his death, Dr. Clifton was recognized by the American Psychological Association as the "Grandfather of Positive Psychology."

Your life is really based on relationships, isn't it? You weren't placed here to live alone like a hermit; you were placed here to interact and build relationships throughout life. Dr. Clifton discovered that your life is defined by your relationships and how you interact with others. He viewed each interaction as having a profound effect on your psyche.

Your emotions are rarely neutral; they are either positive or negative (just like love and fear). The same holds true for your interactions; they, too, are almost always positive or negative. Though you may take these interactions for granted by living in default with an undisciplined mind, they have a cumulative effect on you. Dr. Clifton used a simple analogy involving a bucket and a dipper. Very profound in its simplicity.

How does it work? In a nutshell, everyone has an invisible bucket. It is emptied or filled with each interaction, depending on what others say or do to you. When your "bucket" is filled up, you feel great; when it's empty, you feel lousy. Everyone has an invisible dipper. Whenever you use your dipper to say or do something to increase someone else's positive emotions, you fill their bucket, and your own, at the same time.

Conversely, by saying or doing something to cause negative emotions, you diminish that other person as well as yourself. This is a creative way to discipline your mind to direct the Law of Attraction to really work for you. Dr. Clifton inspired every employee at Gallup to institute this simple conscious philosophy into each interaction.

As a result, his employees developed disciplined minds. He took the age-old saying, "If you can't say something nice about someone else, don't say anything at all," and improved it to, "Say something nice always and nice will happen to you." The Law of Attraction, karma, and The Golden Rule in a new form: a bucket and a dipper.

During the Korean War, imprisonment in the North Korean POW camps resulted in a 38 percent death rate—the highest in U.S. military history. Yet, the prisoners weren't tortured; they were provided adequate food, water, and shelter. In fact, fewer cases of physical abuse were reported in the North Korean POW camps than in prison camps from any other major military conflict throughout history.

How can this be? Why did POWs die? Disease? On the contrary, the captives were provided adequate medical attention. No tsunami either. Run out of reasons? The North Koreans employed the most deadly form of torture—negativity.

After the Korean War, Major (Dr.) William Mayer—who would later become the U.S. Army's chief psychiatrist—studied over a thousand Americans detained as prisoners of war in a North Korean camp. Dr. Mayer discovered that the North Koreans' primary objective was to "deny men the emotional support that comes from interpersonal relationships." They systemically encouraged and rewarded informing (ratting out your fellow U.S. soldier), self-criticism, breaking loyalty to leadership and country, and withholding all positive emotional support.

All positive letters from home were destroyed; only news of negativity was passed along, such as a death in the family, spousal separation, and financial turmoil. In short, they broke the prisoners' spirits with constant negativity, causing them to completely give up mentally, physically, and emotionally. Dr. Clifton was so moved by Dr. Mayer's research that it inspired him to create positive psychology and put his theories into practice.

It stands to reason that applying the Law of Polarity (everything has a polar opposite) the reverse results can happen with an environment of positives. This is exactly what Dr. Clifton was able to do with the Gallup Organization and with the millions of people who implemented the bucket and dipper concept into their workplaces.

Earlier, you read that four out of five people are unhappy in their jobs and that we would examine the one out of five who is happy. Dr. Clifton proved that he could create a culture of happiness, using his bucket and dipper theory. By having employees keep a bucket on their desks and challenging them to consciously become "bucket fillers," he created a workplace where the majority—even more than one out of five—became happy in their jobs. Bucket fillers find bliss in their jobs. It's that simple.

Are you a bucket filler? Do you make others feel positive emotions with the majority of your words and actions? Your bliss is tied to this basic tenet of positive psychology. Become a positive psychologist yourself and you will find your bliss.

Sixty-five percent of Americans receive no recognition in the workplace, says Dr. Clifton in *How Full Is Your Bucket?*

Are You Living the Dream and Saying So?

Whenever someone asks me how I'm doing, I love to enthusiastically answer, "Living the dream." People will look at me funny, half wondering if I am for real or just plain nuts (in my case, both are true).

I can tell a lot about people and where they are in their lives after asking the simple question, "How are you doing?" If the answer is, "Not bad," uh oh, that translates to *bad.* "Can't complain" means *complaining.* "All things considered, I'm okay." Just okay? Not many great things have ever been accomplished with *just okay* ambitions.

How do you answer the question, "How are you doing?" Do you answer, "Not bad," "Can't complain," or "Okay?" Try answering, "Living the dream" and see if the other person looks at you as if you're crazy? Know what's crazy? Actually thinking and, in turn, believing, you are "not bad," or "can't complain," or just "okay."

The point is this: words have tremendous meaning. Your words are actually energy. They are the building block in your energy hierarchy;

it starts with your words, then your thoughts, and culminates with your emotions. Your emotions are guided by your words and then your thoughts. So your emotions are your highest form of energy emitted in the form of a vibration. Think of your emotion as energy in motion.

The more negative you are in your words—as we discussed with four-letter words—the more negative results you will attract. The great news is that your words can also attract what you really want. From now on, answer the question, "How are you doing?" with "Fantastic!" "Great!" "Living the dream!" or "Outstanding!" And mean it.

So many people actually deflate their self image with their own words. At some point, you've probably said, "I'm so stupid" or "I'm such an idiot" or "I'm so clumsy"—you get the point. You rarely hear someone say, "I'm great!"

Bad bosses could increase their employees' risk of stroke by 33 percent, according to the authors of *How Full Is Your Bucket?*

My challenge to you is to take control of your thoughts—with your words. Remember, the more disciplined your mind, the greater your results. Your subconscious cannot discriminate what you say (between *don't* versus *do*), so think before you speak. And make positive affirmations your way of life—your automatic thought.

- "I can't wait for …" only pushes what you say further away from you. Say, "I'm excited for …"
- "I feel lousy" will only make you feel worse. Say, "I feel healthy" and you will start attracting good health.
- "I'm sick" will only worsen your condition. Say, "I'm grateful to feel vibrant and healthy."
- "I don't want to be broke" will bankrupt you eventually (I hear this one a lot). Say, "I wish to be financially independent and abundantly prosperous."

- "I hate this job" becomes, "I'm grateful for the contrast I've learned in this job. I now know what I desire in my next job."
- "I hate my boss" becomes, "I'm grateful for the contrast I've learned from my boss. I now know the type of boss I truly desire and deserve."
- "Life stinks" becomes, "Life's full of bliss."

Words Make Water Smile

Dr. Masaru Emoto examined the effect words have on water. In his book *The Hidden Messages in Water,* Dr. Emoto proved with factual evidence that human vibrational energy, thoughts, words, ideas, and music affect the molecular structure of water. Through high-powered photography, Dr. Emoto published pictures of what water looked like after saying, "Thank you," "Love and appreciation," "Soul," "Love plus gratitude," and "Mother Teresa." The result was amazing: the water was transformed from ordinary form into beautiful crystals.

The polar opposite also held true. Words like "You make me sick—I will kill you," "Adolf Hitler," and "Hate" transformed the water into nasty images. Even polluted, filthy looking water could be transformed into beautiful shapes with positive words. See an analogy here? Mind pollution can be cleared up with the right goals (words that stem from thoughts) which, with enthusiasm and confidence, become you.

Water comprises over 70 percent of a human body and, for that matter, covers the same amount of our planet. Water is the very source of all life on this planet. Its quality and integrity are vitally important to all forms of life. Your body is very much like a sponge and is composed of trillions of chambers called "cells," which hold liquid. The quality of your life is directly connected to the quality of your water. What are toxic words doing to your "body" of water?

You get the picture. I hope this doesn't seem trivial and trite to you because the Law of Attraction is what you make of it. You hold the building blocks, and the area in which you may build is limitless. Your Co-Builder is pulling for you to expand all facets of your life to even greater bliss. Take control of your words, thoughts, and feelings and then your results will resemble beautiful crystals. Every time.

When someone asks you, "How are you doing?" answer "Living the dream!" You may even make them smile.

What's Your Passion (and It's Not about the Money)

*"If you always do what interests you,
at least one person will be pleased."*
Katharine Hepburn

I recently spoke with Eric, a wealthy surgeon who was miserable. He didn't like his job. When I asked why he stayed with it, his answer was, "But it pays the bills!" That wasn't an answer to my question, so I asked again, "Why don't you like your job?"

"The hours are brutal and malpractice insurance is outrageous!" he bemoaned.

I persisted, "Well, what would be your dream job?"

"Huh?"

"What job would make you happy?"

"Well, one with a lot fewer hours."

"Don't you control your own schedule?"

"Yes and no," he said.

"What do you mean?"

"I don't schedule surgeries or appointments."

"Who does?"

"Admin people."

"How many hours do you work in a given day?" I asked him.

"All day long!"

"Describe a typical day?"

"I'm here by 8:30 every day."

"Do you see patients then?"

"My first appointment is usually at 9 AM and my last is done by 6 PM."

"Do you take lunch or any breaks?" I wanted to know.

"I usually skip lunch or eat on the fly between appointments—and FORGET about breaks."

"How many days are you in surgery?"

"Two."

"Weekends?"

"No, thank God. But I bring tons of work home with me."

"What kind of work?"

"Paperwork, x-rays, files."

"When do you have time for your lovely wife?"

"Never. We hardly see each other and when we do, we usually fight, or she just nags me," he said.

Let's examine this scenario for a moment. Here's a guy driving a black Porsche (dream car), living in a mansion overlooking a beautiful, private golf course (dream house), making big bucks with a very attractive wife (dream spouse) and three great kids (dream family). He's brilliant. On the surface, he has it all. And yet, he is bankrupt inside. Why is he miserable in his job? Well, it's not about the money. And his misery in his job infects his relationship with his spouse, his kids, and, most importantly, with himself.

He was feeling drained and stressed out to the max. He looked ten years older than he was, complete with bags under his eyes, as he sat there moaning. He was having his own pity party right in front of me. By now, you know my advice (it's tough to feel any pity for a man with so many obvious blessings). But his problems were real—to him. His problems were all attitudinal and his attitude stunk! He was allowing his schedule to drain him further. In fact, he could control his own schedule if he truly wanted to.

Obviously, it wasn't really the schedule (8:30–6, Monday to Friday). It was his attitude. He was rationalizing his business. Said another way, he was *RATION-LIES-ing* his *BUSY-NESS*. He felt overworked, therefore, he was overworked. He blamed others when there really was only one place for any blame—inside. His glass was empty. He was caging himself in. And, ironically, he had the keys to unlock his own cage and to re-discover his own freedom. It started with gratitude, which was completely missing in his psyche.

A dream job is a relational experience—knowing you are doing something that makes the world a better place. There are three primary forms of relationships: (1) self, (2) others, and (3) environment. My friend was zero for three. He wasn't taking care of himself physically, mentally, or emotionally. He did not love himself.

This lack of love of self carried over into relationships with others; he was constantly complaining and miserable to be around. His relationship with environment was a failure also. He couldn't see beauty in anything. He complained that his house wasn't enough and that he was sick of the weather and he wasn't making enough money. He was a taker, not a giver; a victim, not a grateful professional living in financially abundant prosperity.

I asked him why he chose to become a doctor. He said, "My dad was a doctor and he always made good money so I just figured since I had good enough grades, I could become a doctor too."

Time for an assessment of my friend the miserable doctor:

- The motivation for his job was based on heredity and not on what he was passionate about (chances are his father wasn't happy either). His father always said to him, "I want you to become a doctor," but my friend never truly said, "I want to become a doctor." When others make your decisions, don't be surprised when they backfire.

- Money was the driving force behind his job choice. He is not alone; most people in professional jobs list money as one of the top reasons for choosing their particular profession. Yet, why are so many professionals—doctors, lawyers, accountants, dentists, and executives—unhappy? After all, they rank money number one, and they make plenty of the green stuff. Money alone is clearly not their workplace joystick.

You are a spiritual being living in a physical world. Your essence, your real driving force as a spiritual being, is in your three primary relationships: self, others, and environment. This means feeling appreciated by others and appreciating your own self and the world around you. Your true inner core is love, joy, wisdom, and abundance. If you cling to a material possession like money on a cosmic level, that alone cannot bring true happiness.

Ever visit someone on their death bed? They never say, "Oh, if only I made another hundred grand." Rather, they say, "Tell so and so I love them." It's about relationships. Mother Teresa said it well: "Even the rich are hungry for love, for being cared for, for being wanted, for having someone to call their own."

There is another reason why money alone doesn't bring happiness. Often, the focus is on scarcity—on lack of money. The negative thought, "I don't have enough money"—even if you are bringing in six or even seven figures—actually causes you to never have enough of that green stuff. And, after a while, this becomes a pattern (paradigm) that perpetuates itself. Unless the focus is on abundance and financial independence, your energies are focused on scarcity. The Universe responds to your vibration with poof: scarcity city!

Passion means finding the vocation that feels like a vacation—the point when time does stand still for you—when you are in a zone. And here's the rub: only you know your blissful dream job. Your parents, teachers, clergy, buddies, or spouse—even though they may seem to know you, they don't know. You now understand that external forces only pull you away from your inner self if you are not careful.

The Geeks Have the Last Laugh

Some of the most interesting and important people throughout time were considered outcasts—today we'd refer to them as "geeks." Aristotle, Jesus, Gandhi, Shakespeare, Galileo, Einstein, Beethoven, Abe Lincoln, and Henry Ford, to name a few, were considered by "proper society" to be outcasts. Many of them were even brutally killed for their beliefs.

Their common trait? An unyielding inner strength and total confidence in what they believed in. Whether it was composing music, leading people to freedom, dying for the forgiveness of mankind's sins, building a car, or visualizing a new scientific discovery, all these people were true to their inner voice—their passion.

When we are connected with our inner wisdom, we are in our dream job state. Even if others call you a geek, it doesn't matter. If someone is trying to disconnect you from your inner harmony, then he or she is the true geek.

Remember, mediocrity attacks excellence, and if you are going to pursue your dreams, your social life may change. Friends will likely question you and may even belittle you for your desired aspirations. Henry Ford's "friends" tried to have him committed to a mental institution because of his passion for building the first commercial automobile. Where do you think Ford's friends were: in challenge mode or sitting idle?

I'm glad Ford had the courage to ignore his so-called friends. Are your friends likely to want you to stay idle with them? Don't be surprised. As you rise to a higher plane in life, you will need to leave behind any toxic friends and peers—anyone who tries to hold you back. Bosses, friends, coworkers, family, and peers may not handle your quest for the new you (complete with lofty dreams) very well. You will learn that if they do not support you, then they're not friends, but foes. Good riddance.

There is a simple yet powerful phrase that Dr. Emile Coué developed and integrated into his patients' psyche during hypnosis with thousands of documented cures for a variety of ailments: "Negative thoughts, negative suggestions, have no influence over me at any level of mind."

A very powerful statement when committed to your subconscious. If you don't allow mean-spirited criticism to infect the "new you," it will boomerang back to its originator. Hard!

Another phrase Dr. Coué is best known for, and also used to help heal thousands of documented patients, was this one: "Every day, in every way, I am getting better, better, and better."

This is equally powerful when committed into the subconscious under hypnosis. The good news: you don't need a hypnotist to benefit from these powerful phrases, through a technique I explain in the next section.

Fortunately, Aristotle, Jesus, Gandhi, Mother Teresa, Galileo, Shakespeare, Lincoln, and Ford were unswayed from their bliss by others. When mediocrity (in other words, idleness) attacks excellence (the new you) say, "Thank you *for-giving* me the experience," and don't succumb to outside forces and pressures.

Check out one of the richest people in the world, the founder of Microsoft—Bill Gates. There is a classic picture of Gates, just after dropping out of Harvard, with a burning dream for software applications and concepts, posing with his future partners. One word comes to mind when you look at the young Bill Gates (hint, it starts with a *G*).

How to Solve a Problem with No Effort

What if I told you solving problems is so easy that you could do it in your sleep. Would you try it? Sure you would.

By now, you know how powerful your subconscious mind is. You can tap into the infinite wisdom you already possess inside of you and harness it to solve your problems—in your sleep. Literally. That's right, you can use your dreams to help you solve a problem. With a little practice (so there is some effort needed) in "programming your dreams," you can become quite proficient. You will be amazed at how powerful this tool can be.

It's simple. Just do this: right before you fall asleep for the night, say to yourself, "I desire to have a dream that will contain information to solve (state your problem)."

Then, after stating the problem, say to yourself, "I will have such a dream, remember it, and understand it." Just as before, feel as if the problem is already solved—with confidence. Feel the gratitude you will experience for receiving the solution through your dream as if it has already happened. This is important.

Enhance the likelihood for success in controlling your dreams by meditation. While in the alpha state (a deep phase of meditation when your brain waves slow down; you're in "the zone"), visualize the problem and mentally say, "I want to remember a dream of importance. I will remember a dream." Ideally, meditate just before you sleep.

After you "program" your dream, all you have to do is fall asleep. When you awaken—either in the middle of the night or in the morning, and before you do anything (you will likely still be in the alpha state of consciousness—the best way to retrieve the dream), write down everything you remember from your most vivid dream (keep a notepad and pen bedside).

Then, search your notes for meaning. With patience and total belief, it will work. It may take a few nights before you start remembering your dreams. Stick with it. You will be amazed by what your dreams will tell you. The only caution is to search for answers for something important. Trivial problems usually get trivial answers.

At this point, you may be skeptical and even start calling me names. Well, I'll be okay: negative thoughts, negative suggestions, have no influence over me at any level of mind. What if I could give you an example of a famous product that was "invented" through a dream? How about the sewing machine?

Elias Howe was trying to invent a machine that could sew clothing. Sewing by hand was tedious, time-consuming, and expensive. He knew there was a way, but was completely stumped and was racking his brain. He had a burning desire to solve this problem—he knew there had to be a method, but his mind was stuck. Then, he had a vivid dream—and remembered it: *A man was in a jungle surrounded by savages. They were coming menacingly close to him, their spears rising, then descending. Each spear had a hole in the tip.*

When Howe awakened, he knew this dream solved his burning question to the problem and, voilà, he designed the sewing machine. Earlier, he could make the needle rise and descend, but not sew—until his dream told him to put the hole at the tip.

Quite a bit has been written about dream interpretation. Sigmund Freud was a pioneer in the subject. Don't get Freud's work confused with our application. Freud's patients did not program their dreams; they just had dreams and remembered them.

One of your greatest challenges is to have a disciplined mind, not an undisciplined mind. You are deliberately programming your dreams for a specific purpose, not just dreaming in default. Big difference. See a parallel with the development of your (conscious) mind? Programming your time (having a disciplined, focused mind) is also how you succeed while you are awake.

If Howe had not deliberately programmed his dream, we would not have the sewing machine. Back to Siggy. Imagine how Freud would have interpreted Howe's dream? (I couldn't pass that one up.)

If you can program yourself into a disciplined mind 24/7 (while sleeping and awake), imagine what you are capable of accomplishing? If you are struggling with "what's my true dream job?" try programming your dreams for an answer.

I use dream programming all the time in my search business. Recently, a new client hired me to find a VP of Sales for them. Their headquarters was in a city that wasn't exactly in the top ten most desirable cities—even in their eyes. They were resigned to the fact that they would have a tough time getting someone to move to their undesirable location. My database didn't turn up anybody in the general area of their headquarters on the first try, so rather than panic, that night I programmed a dream to give me clear guidance of where to look.

When I awakened the next morning, my first thought was to call a guy I had known for years—let's call him Matt. I hadn't spoken to Matt for a few months, but for some reason, I knew I had to call him that morning, and, at first, I was worried that he might be in trouble.

When I called Matt, he answered on the first ring. He said, "It's funny you called—I was just thinking of calling you" (I could hear the theme from the *Twilight Zone*). In the past, Matt would never consider relocating out of the Northeast. On this particular day, as Matt told me he was open to relocating to the Southeast (where the position was), I was stunned—was this the same guy?

I said, "I have a great opportunity there right now." Just after I told him the name of the city, Matt interrupted me and said, "You know my oldest son is going there on a baseball scholarship?"

With tingling up and down my spine, I blurted out, "Oh yeah … that's right." As he Google-mapped the headquarters address, he discovered the company was only one mile from the campus.

There are no coincidences. The job was exactly what Matt was looking for—his dream job. I sent him in on the first interview. The client absolutely loved him! I placed him in the job with ease, and he is eternally grateful that I called him with the opportunity. He had no idea how easy it was to think of him—I followed my dream "hunch." I later called Matt and explained what had happened, and he now understands and practices the Law of Attraction. Now, he even programs his dreams too.

Start tonight. Instead of wishing someone sweet dreams, how about wishing that person to have productive dreams.

You Control Your Bliss

"The weak have remedies, the wise have joys;
superior wisdom is superior bliss."
Edward Young

I have thrown a lot of information at you, and I'm sure your head is spinning a little. If so, this is good. Challenge begets growth. As you have developed your *Bliss List*, you have gained superior wisdom. There was no point in jumping to the résumé section before you created your *Bliss List*, established your positive attitude, and dreamed about your dream job.

Any goal you set with enthusiastic confidence, becomes reality. The key to attracting your bliss lies in understanding and applying the amazing universal Law of Attraction. In order to attract your blissful dream job, you have to raise your energy (vibration) and be disciplined enough to keep it raised. You guide your thoughts and emotions. You reach for a feeling. Your spirit (subconscious) has domain over your mind, which has domain over your body. You can reach your spirit through meditation, programming your dreams, and by purifying your thoughts with positive emotion and matching, effective language.

There are plenty of helpful gimmicks to use to help you obtain your bliss, and I have given you some of them: Bliss Lists, Bliss Jars, Bliss Boards, Bliss Cards, for examples. Beyond these helpful techniques, the essence of your bliss is you: "re-membering" your inner spirit. The real trick is for you to turbo-charge your energy toward obtaining your goals with enthusiastic confidence and gratitude. You choose your emotional state; you choose how you allocate your time. And you have your blissful dream job already inside you. Your challenge is to "remember" it.

I am often asked, "How can I raise my vibration and attract my blissful dream job?" The following is a recap of several suggestions, some mentioned earlier, with a few new ones to keep it fresh.

- Gratitude. Gratitude. Gratitude. The glass is not half full or half empty; it's always full—especially if you apply gratitude to everything. Start your day with gratitude and continue your day with gratitude. Develop an attitude of gratitude.
- Meditation. Meditate three times per day for fifteen minutes per session (see the box nearby; I give you a simple way to meditate).
- Music. Listen to Beethoven's *Pastorale* and any classical music that ignites your soul.
- Exercise. Your body produces natural drugs that make you feel "high"—and they're free and legal.
- Seminars. Make the time to recharge your batteries; travel to an interesting place—it's well worth it.
- Attend religious services. Just entering into a place of worship will usually lift your spirits. Find the ones that inspire you (not make you feel guilty) and spend an hour.
- Be happy. Think about what makes you happy, and remember it when you are not.
- Comedy. Laughter from movies or "live" comedy are great ways to get in a good mood.
- Read a book that inspires you. Reread the ones that have most inspired you. It's like riding a bike; the more you read and reread (practice), the more automatic the message will become. I list the most profound books that have influenced me in a section at the back of this book called Read More, if you'd like some suggestions.
- Get a massage. Go to a spa.
- Dance. Sing. Sing and dance.

- Do yoga.
- Go for a scenic bike ride.
- Hike in the mountains. Go for a walk. Drive a scenic route.
- Sit on a park bench and listen to the birds singing and the children laughing.
- Pray.
- Hold a puppy or a kitten.
- Rest. Never underestimate the power of a power nap.
- Think about your goals—put 'em on your walls, in your wallet/ purse, in a jar, and in your mind. It all works. Visualize your dream job.
- Watch the *Planet Earth* DVD in surround sound.
- Keep yourself in a positive emotional state: first, for five minutes, then for a half hour, then an hour, and then all day long. Feel gratitude, joy, love, passion, enthusiasm, happiness, optimism, hope, wisdom, contentment, and peace throughout the day.
- Get in "The Now," that place where you are truly present, where guilt (past) and fear (future) cannot exist.
- Take deep breaths using your stomach. Inhale through your nose and exhale through your mouth.
- Watch the sun rise. Watch the sun set (notice how they both look different each time).
- Tell someone, "I love you"—and mean it.
- Have wild passionate lovemaking (wanted to see if you were still paying attention!).
- Relive your happiest childhood memory in your mind.
- Attend the symphony. Listen to the majestic beauty. Then close your eyes and get to the alpha level—and listen to the difference.

- Say hello to perfect strangers. When you say hello, smile. You use a lot fewer muscles to smile than to frown.
- Hold the door open for a perfect stranger.

How to Meditate

Though it may be easier to lie down, it's not necessary. All you need to do is close your eyes, turn your gaze upward at about 20 degrees and focus on your breathing.

Breathe using your stomach and not your chest. Take deep, slow breaths. Just focus on your inhaling and exhaling. Keep focusing on your breathing; don't allow your mind to drift off.

If you find yourself thinking about something else, recognize it but don't engage. Just say, "Cancel," and bring yourself back to focusing on your breathing. With a little practice, this form of meditation will become easy for you and can be used anywhere.

Most of us are too busy to set aside time to meditate. You can put mindful meditation into your day. Here are some suggestions:

- Pay attention to your breathing or your environment when you stop at red lights.
- Before you go to sleep, and when you awaken, take some "mindful" breaths.
- Instead of allowing your mind to wander over the day's concerns, direct your attention to your breathing.
- Find a task that you do impatiently or unconsciously (standing in line or brushing your teeth, for example) and concentrate on the experience.
- Make something that occurs several times during a day, such as answering the phone or buckling your seatbelt, a reminder to return to the present—that is, think about what you're doing and observe yourself doing it.

Can you think of any people who have blissful dream jobs? There are plenty of famous people who have said they love their jobs—who are in the *Bliss Zone*: Oprah Winfrey, Warren Buffett, Jimmy Buffett, Henry Ford, Thomas Edison, Albert Einstein, Beethoven, William Shakespeare, John Grisham, Jose Silva, Bill Gates, Michael Jordan, Doug Flutie, Steven Spielberg, Walt Disney, Katharine Hepburn, Tiger Woods, Jack Canfield, James Taylor, and Ronald Reagan, to name a few.

Each of these people is known for exuding confidence and being positive thinkers. Each has transcended his or her dreams into blissful dream jobs.

Finding bliss in a dream job is not limited to celebrity—it's also the guy who loves to wait on tables and makes your meal entertaining with his energy; it's the Disney tour guide who exudes joy in describing the place; it's the artist sitting in front of a scene, entranced with capturing the view on canvas. All these people have found their bliss and are *living the dream.* You can too. If you are not, I hope this section helped you understand why not; most importantly, you now know *you* control everything in your life—with your disciplined mind.

I mentioned some famous people who were/are in dream jobs and had some examples of regular people (such as the waiter, tour guide, and artist). One of my best examples, though, is my mother. She was the perfect 1950s housewife. My dad was the successful lawyer—the bread winner; my mom, the housewife. She raised four kids (raising me was like raising five), cooked every dinner like a chef, and ran an immaculate house (not an easy task with my two sisters). Think *Leave It to Beaver*: my mother was June Cleaver.

She accepted her "lot in life" gracefully, but I could tell doing the mundane homemaker duties wasn't her dream job. She was a voracious reader (the apple doesn't fall far from the tree); she loved volunteering for public television; she loved entertaining and laughing; and she even loved being a Den Mother for Cub Scouts. Her *Bliss List* probably wouldn't have had "changing diapers," "slaving over a stove," or "driving four kids all over town for sports/activities." But she accepted her role. After we kids started moving out to college, things changed for my mother.

As the empty-nester phase was nearing, my mother developed her dream job. She and another "former housewife" and friend partnered in forming a company, which they named *Color & You*. They each worked out of their own homes and became clothing consultants. They used some scientific research (you look your best in the colors of one of the four "seasons"—such as winter, spring, summer, or fall) and marketed their ability to determine what looked best on their clients, plus they sold their own hypoallergenic, high-quality, makeup line.

The book *Dress for Success* had been a bestseller, so people were interested in looking their best for interviews and at work. My mother saw an opportunity and took action. *Color & You* was successful and became her dream job.

So if you are a homemaker or stay-at-home mom and perhaps feeling trapped in life, after reading this book, I hope this story inspires you to follow your intuitive dreams. A blissful dream job can—and does—happen later in life. My mother's story was early inspiration for me to write this book. (In case you're wondering, I'm a summer, body type "C." I look my best in solid, pastel, blue-based colors.)

The purpose of this section is to awaken you. In the beginning, I said that you control your bliss. By now, you are convinced—and it is incredibly empowering to know that you control your destiny. I hope you are now using all the helpful tricks and exercises discussed, but ultimately, it is you and only you who knows what's best for you—your blissful dream job.

The purpose of this more spiritual side or mystical third of this book was also to prepare you for the practical action phase next. As you worked through the material, you may have had some negative thoughts that might have hindered you, causing angst in your life and in your work. Being able to guide your thoughts and align your subconscious with your conscious mind is the key to obtaining your dream job.

Positive thoughts with positive emotions bring positive results.

Now, it's time for the practical—putting your desires into action by using your disciplined, positive mind.

3

The Résumé:
Your Invisible
First Impression

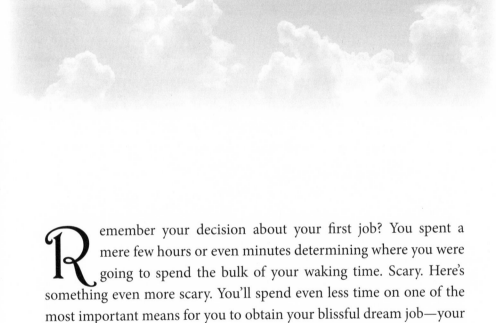

Remember your decision about your first job? You spent a mere few hours or even minutes determining where you were going to spend the bulk of your waking time. Scary. Here's something even more scary. You'll spend even less time on one of the most important means for you to obtain your blissful dream job—your résumé.

You know the importance of a good first impression. Yet very few people spend enough time on their true first impression—their résumés. Believe me, I've seen plenty of lousy résumés—some I'll share soon. These people didn't think of their résumé as their first impression. This mindset (a real hindrance) will only keep them stuck in the mud and certainly not propel them into a blissful dream job.

Your résumé is your invisible first impression. And it goes without saying how important first impressions are.

The One-Page Myth

I had an executive level manager—we'll call him Jim—argue with me trying to defend his single-page (and inadequate) résumé. After college, he had worked for three blue-chip companies. He had a consistent track record of achievement and the promotions to show for it, accounting for a total of seven jobs in fourteen years of professional experience. Impressive background—and perfect for the job I was hoping to place him in.

Jim should have been a no-brainer for the Vice President job my firm was retained to fill. He had all the qualifications and then some—but they were not on paper (first impression). In my opinion, Jim had short-changed his career by shoe-horning it into only one page.

The result: I presented his résumé to my client whose first words were, "Looks light." (No kidding!)

Sometimes, that's all it takes to derail your opportunity to interview and lose a potential dream job. Since this particular client was a personal friend of many years, I attempted to push back with, "Oh, it's only a résumé. You will really like this guy!" I didn't sound too convincing.

"Who else do you have?" he replied with a disturbed tone.

There wasn't much more I could do except to slide Jim in with other candidates—later. I knew if I could just get him in front of the hiring manager, he would nail it—in spite of his lame résumé. This entire dilemma was due to his wimpy, one-page résumé—creating a poor first impression.

Unless you spend the time necessary to give yourself a positive first impression with an attention-grabbing résumé that rocks (I'll help make the process easier than you think), you may as well resign yourself to the fact that you'll never be given the opportunity. On my wall, I have a saying, "Success means being ready when opportunity knocks." Having the best résumé you possibly can is being ready for that opportunity and leads to success.

I'm frequently asked, "What is the best résumé format?" You could ask ten people this question and may very well get ten different answers. The best résumé is one that moves yours to the top of the pile with the hiring manager. How? After years of trial and error, I have formulated an ideal résumé format that works. First, I'll describe it and then later give you some examples and a template.

The best résumé covers two areas: (1) activities and (2) accomplishments in chronological order, beginning with your most recent job. Use sentences in paragraph form for the activities and bullet points to highlight your accomplishments.

Some résumé advisers say you should do your résumé in the form of a letter. My answer: if that's what your dream company wants, that's what you do, but the most widely accepted résumé is still done chronologically by job/company.

Many times, a recruiter may do his or her own "write up" about you in lieu of your résumé. Make it easy by having a strong chronological résumé with clear descriptions of what you do/did and what you accomplished. This should give a recruiter enough ammo to present your qualifications with enthusiasm.

Ready to begin? First off, don't feel as if you have to pay a résumé service to do your résumé for you. Résumé services tend to follow templates that lack individuality. Don't defer your dream job quest to an outside service. Write it yourself. Use Microsoft Word if you have it. Word is the most accepted business software. Chances are, a résumé service would type it on Word anyway. As another bonus, doing it yourself gives you the very important option of altering and tailoring your content to fit your target dream companies.

When listing your name at the top of the first page, use your nickname (the name you go by) rather than your full legal name. This adds a little warmth to the start and avoids your having to ask the hiring manager to call you something else right off the bat (first impressions). There's a big difference in listing *Daniel Arthur Worthington, III* vs. *Dan Worthington.*

Paragraph Your Activities

This is the mundane but necessary part of your résumé.

- In the first line, describe your primary, overall responsibility. What geography you cover, how many employees you manage, any clients you are directly responsible for, and anything that may be pertinent to companies you are targeting. For example, *responsible for $100 million in annual sales in the eastern United States for a 550-item pet food manufacturer.*
- Next, describe your company's reporting and operational structure. *Report to the Vice President of Sales, oversee a direct sales force at headquarters and a brokerage force at retail. Supervise 100 employees through eight direct reports: five Region Managers, two Divisional Category Managers and one Administrative Assistant.*
- If you are directly responsible for any customers, especially large, recognizable ones, indicate them by name.
- If you were able to obtain a position description for your target job, include anything that pertains to what the company is looking for in your background. Interject any applicable responsibilities accordingly. For example, if company x is looking for a people manager, include how many employees you manage and list their titles.

- Do not fill your paragraph with flowery verbiage such as *while keeping the company's best interests in mind.* Keep it clear and concise. Fewer syllables wins you points with the interviewer.

Bullet Point Your Accomplishments

Bullet points are the most important element of your entire résumé. And, ironically, typically the format item most résumé writers forget to use. You actually learned about bullet points in your Advertising 101 class. Any time you can use objects in a presentation (a résumé is a presentation of you), the impact is far greater than merely with words. The reader is more likely to remember items highlighted with an object.

Your Advertising 101 class taught you that, ideally, you would use colored objects in a presentation, but, like the objects example, that's not sound advice for your résumé. Notwithstanding colored objects, bullet points are effective and easy to use (one click on the old toolbar). They draw the reader to your accomplishments. Using my bullet-point advice will catapult your résumé to the "must see" pile.

What is it you want to bullet point? Accomplishments such as these:

- Increases in revenue
  (if double digit—more on this in a minute)
- Decreases in expenses
- Awards won
- Bonuses earned
- Rank vs. peers (especially if it's a #1)
- New innovative technique(s) designed by you
  and used by others
- Buzz words important to the target company

- Leadership/task forces, especially if chosen by senior management
- Teamwork
- Hiring, promoting employees
- Restructuring to improve efficiency

Bullet points must be believable yet impressive. How can you make them believable? Quantify and qualify—and without any passive words. Avoid using words such as *implement, execute,* or *follow.* The language in your bullet-pointed accomplishments should reflect strength and confidence. Use these strong words: *created, designed, led, obtained, ranked #1, awarded,* and so on. The following is a bullet-point example:

- Implemented sales programs

versus

- Increased sales by 31.6% in FY 2008, +37.3% in FY 2007, and + 32.1% in FY 2006

Which bullet point is more effective? "Implemented sales programs" is too vague and is something anyone could say. It says, "I drop off the stuff other people wrote for me to say." In short: it underwhelms the reader.

The second bullet point quantifies (31.6%, 37.3%, and 32.1%) and qualifies (FY 2008, 2007, 2006). It is believable because of its precision and it is impressive—you always want to use double digits for increases.

What if you didn't have double digit increases? Well, you have to be creative. Not many employers say, "Get me some salespeople who can drive some stagnant, single-digit increases." Let's say your increases were a modest +3.2% in '08, +4.2% in '07 and +3.8% in '06. Your bullet point would be

- Increased sales by 11.2% vs. industry average of +5.1%

I would advise you to leave out the three singular years and instead add them together, since you were in the job three years. And we added the "industry average" number, so the reader can see you more than doubled the industry average. It is still impressive and believable (quantified and qualified). Much more so than "Implemented sales programs."

Tailor your accomplishments to your target company's hot buttons. Place yourself in their shoes and brainstorm your most applicable successes. Be creative. List them in order of importance, with the top bullet point being the most important.

Which ones are the most important? The accomplishments most sought after by all companies are

- Increasing revenues
- Decreasing expenses
- Increasing efficiencies

I'm going to repeat this point from earlier: quantify and qualify.

- Be specific.
- Avoid flowery verbiage.
- Use action verbs.

Be deliberate in marketing yourself. If you seek a position that will emphasize people development, list the number of employees you have developed and promoted.

Try to limit the number of bullet points to five for your most recent (and most important) position and three or fewer for earlier positions. Don't dilute your bullet points. Less is more here. Five impactful bullet points stand out and get the reader excited; eleven blend in and lose their impact, not to mention the reader.

The average time the interviewer will spend on your résumé is less than one minute. Less than one minute! Hit home runs with your bullet points. Ask your executive recruiter, "What is most important to the hiring manager?" and tailor your bullet points accordingly.

A candidate once told me—in trying to defend his weak résumé (and the fact that he was too lazy to re-do it)—that he didn't want to "give too much information on the résumé, or there wouldn't be anything to talk about in the interview." Wrong-O! A lousy résumé won't get you the interview. If properly written, though, a résumé can allow you to focus on chemistry with the interviewer versus explaining (that is, defending) your background. The following tips will help your résumé shine:

Length

If you follow the recommended chronological, paragraph, and bullet point format, your résumé should be as long as it needs to be. One-page résumés place you at a disadvantage, yet some people still believe a résumé should be one page (Procter & Gamble teaches this—probably so their employees don't get interviewed.).

The one-pager is realistic for a recent college graduate; the more experience you have, the longer your résumé should be. If your résumé is clear, concise, and well-written, length should be a non-issue. So, length really doesn't matter (just wanted to see if you were still alert).

Contents

Sections entitled "Objectives" and "Career Summaries" are redundant and do not belong on a résumé. A well-written cover letter should serve as your career summary. The very fact that you are interested in this particular position means it is your objective.

Your résumé should include these headings:

- Professional Experience
- Education (all degrees—undergraduate and graduate, with grades listed if at least or higher than 3.0/4.0)
- Honors (if applicable)
- Professional Affiliations (if applicable)
- Additional Training
- Personal (optional)

If your target dream company is looking for a well-adjusted employee (defined as married with children in business circles), by all means, list it; if you're living in a van down by the river and are thrice divorced, do not include.

Some Résumé Don'ts

No picture of yourself (I've seen 'em) and no flowery verbiage. As a rule, if it can be stated with fewer words and syllables, do it. Think technical writing here. Don't use colored paper or cheap copier paper. Cotton-bound white paper is always a winner.

A confusing résumé, littered with typos will land you in the waste basket (round file). Fast. Take the time to proofread your résumé before it is printed! One of the best resources available is already in your computer—spell-check. Use it.

Don't think spell-check alone will suffice. You need to fine-tooth-comb your résumé, word for word. Yours truly sent out 750 résumés to all of my targeted recruiting firms with the word *manger*. Guess what, spell-check let it go because *manger* is a word. But *manger* would have better described the nativity scene than the fact that I was a *manager*. Oops!

My eyes alone didn't catch this glaring typo. So, in addition to your careful proofreading, ask trusted colleagues and friends to critique your résumé for you. You only get one chance, and your first impression has to be perfect.

At the end of this book, in a section called Résumé Makeovers, I use some actual résumés from people with whom I have worked. I will show the "before" and "after" to help illustrate the differences between a résumé that will get placed in the round file (usually crumpled up) versus those moved to the top of the pile. Though the names have been altered, the basic content is verbatim.

4

I Have a Killer Résumé, Now What?

Once you've developed a killer résumé, and you feel confident that potential employers will be equally impressed, it's time to market yourself.

"What is the best marketing strategy?" I'm often asked by candidates. That's a loaded question to ask a recruiter—a "headhunter" will usually just say, "Work exclusively with me!" That's not what is best for you though. You don't ask a barber if you need a haircut. You don't ask a stock broker if you need to change your portfolio. So don't ask a headhunter for advice on your marketing strategy (I'll discuss working with recruiters in the next chapter).

The best marketing strategy is this:
1. Network, network, network
2. Direct mail/email targeted dream companies
3. Direct mail/email targeted executive recruiters

Networking plays the most important practical part in finding your ideal job. Think of people you know and how they can help you: former bosses, colleagues, classmates, alumni, friends, family, neighbors, members of organizations (both social and professional), and members of your religious affiliation. The trick is to cast a wide net. The more effectively you network, the more likely your bliss occupation will happen—don't wait for it to present itself to you.

Add a Killer Cover Letter

Regarding direct mail (snail mail) and email, prepare a professional one-page cover letter that you will attach to your new killer résumé. This letter is important—it's how you market yourself. Think hook, line, and sinker.

What is the best way to interest the recipient of your letter? How can you move him or her to action—to place your résumé on the top of the pile and not in the round file?

- If you can, mention an inside connection—"I was referred by so-and-so-whom-you-respect." Your chances of being seen greatly improve.
- Always provide related experiences and advantages that you bring to the hiring manager and the target company.
- Send your letter to the highest ranking person you can—ideally, the chairman or CEO. The top-down approach works magically—even though the chairman likely isn't to be the person who is responsible for interviewing and hiring you, having the chairman forward your information with his or her approval (either directly or implied) gets you seen. Usually quickly.

- Never, ever, send direct mail with no name or title (do not say this: *To: HR Department* or with the ever-lame: *To Whom It May Concern*). It is a sure-fire way to get tossed in the round file.

Email or Snail Mail?

Which is better: direct mail or email?

Email is actually a more effective way than sending a letter through the regular mail to market yourself to a dream company. Most managers at least glance at each email; whereas, direct mail is more likely to be stacked somewhere—for a prolonged period.

But there is an even more creative way to reach someone: send via FedEx. Almost every FedEx package is opened and read by the recipient. It is expensive (compared to a postage stamp) but very effective. Delivery-service letters and packages (whether DHL, FedEx, or UPS, even USPS Express Mail) require a signature that gets your direct mail in the right person's hands.

Most hiring managers feel that if someone shelled out $20 to $30 to FedEx them a letter and résumé, it must be important enough to read. Getting your résumé in the hands of the intended person is the purpose. If landing you an ideal job costs you $30, isn't the return on investment worth it?

If you send a hard copy (snail mail or FedEx) first, then follow-up via email a week or two later. Both direct mail and electronic mail are effective ways to market yourself, and the combination is even better. This is true whether you are targeting a dream company directly or trying to reach an executive search firm.

What about applying through the target company's website? If you are applying for a specific opening that was listed on the website, go for it. You will not reach the chairman—more likely your letter and résumé will land in the Inbox of a junior human resources person, but it's worth a try. A better approach is applying through the website and then referencing the opening you saw with a targeted FedEx to a senior manager.

Don't get discouraged if your phone doesn't ring off the hook after a direct mail/email marketing effort. The replies you receive will be less than 5 percent on average; remember, the wider you effectively cast your net, the more likely you will be to land that blissful dream job. Ready for some practical advice?

Control the Controllables

What are controllables? They are creating the most professional and effective cover letter and résumé that you possibly can, researching whom you should send it to, and where it should be sent.

Most companies have a web page that contains the mailing address, emails, and information about the management team by title. Plan on sending your cover letter and résumé to the highest ranking person in your target company.

The following is a sample cover letter to be sent to an employer:

Shelly Johnson
110 First Way
Alexandria, VA 22306
(802) 555-5544
Shelly.Johnson@home.com

Mr. Henry Fodora
Ideal Company, Inc.
100 Fifth Avenue
New York, NY 10001

Dear Mr. Fodora,

Nancy Smith of Golden Associates Advertising suggested I contact you regarding the possible public relations opening in your firm.

As an editor and writer for Alexandria's city magazine, I've developed my talent and experience as a public relations writer. Because the staff is very small, I've worn a number of hats, including developing the editorial format and individual story concepts, writing numerous articles, editing copy, laying out the magazine, and supervising production.

Prior to my current position, I was highly involved in the public relations industry, working for Handley & Pratt, where I prepared numerous press releases and media guides, as well as managing several major direct mail campaigns.

My high degree of motivation has been recognized by my previous employers who have quickly promoted me to positions of greater responsibility. I was promoted from assistant editor to editor of *Alexandria Monthly* after only six months.

I am eager to talk with you about the contribution I could make to your firm. I will call you the week of May 21st to see if we can find a mutual time and date to get together and discuss the possibility.

Your consideration is greatly appreciated.

Cordially,
Shelly Johnson

By all means, send a killer cover letter with your résumé even if there is no posted opening. If you do not receive a response within two weeks, call to follow up. Leave only one voicemail message, but keep calling until the employer answers the phone. Be prepared for a mini-interview.

Finally, employ what you learned in the first section of this book: use visualization and focus your positive thinking on obtaining your bliss. The result is worth much more than the effort.

5

Don't Call Us Headhunters or We'll Chop Off Your Head

I offer a unique perspective about executive recruiters. Why? Because I am an executive recruiter. I am living my dream as President of an executive search firm for over fifteen years. Even better, I have been on both sides of the desk as interviewer and interviewee.

Job searchers often ask me, "How did you become a recruiter?" Ironically, it was while working as an employee, and later as an employer, that I began to desire to enter the world of recruiting.

I was fortunate to have gained these interesting perspectives throughout my thirty-one-year career (so far, and I'm far from even thinking about retiring). While I was with a Fortune 100 company, it publicly announced that the division I was in was being divested, so the company had a reason to help us land other employment (and they paid for it). For the first time in my career, I was able to talk to every recruiter that I possibly could without hurting my career. My bosses even referred me to recruiters.

In about seven months, I was able to speak to over 200 recruiters. Of those, I found only two that I had any professional respect for. Some were downright tacky. I had one call my wife "Toots" (I'm not joking, and she sure didn't think it was funny!). You can usually tell in the first few minutes if the recruiter is professional or not.

At the time, the average recruiting firm earned over $375,000 per year—many were one- or two-person shops. The money was good, yet the level of service was poor: lousy follow-up, lack of understanding of the client or the position, and poor communication skills. I said, "Hmm, I can do that." And about three years later, I did!

I had an advantage that many so-called headhunters didn't have. I had experience and training in staffing, managing (but not *manging*), and building businesses. Every job I would recruit for, I had already done. Being a Vice President with a Fortune 31 company gave me instant credibility with candidates and clients. Many of the headhunters had never done anything else other than paper-pushing and headhunting in their lives—and it was obvious!

Tip #1: Don't call a recruiter a *headhunter* if you want him or her to actually help you. Use the term *recruiter* or, better still, *executive search consultant.*

Every job has seemingly morphed into euphemisms. Stewardess became Flight Attendant; Used Car Salesman became Previously Owned Vehicle Sales Executive; and Cashiers became Client Service Representatives. Executive recruiters are still referred to as headhunters. Some even call themselves that. I like to think of myself as a Mystic Career Guide and Life Coach and, thanks to this book, instead of author or writer, I'm now an Inspirational Written-Entertainment Facilitator.

Types of Recruiters

In the past (more than thirty years ago) recruiters were paid by the job seeker (that is, by the candidate). The recruiter would be paid by the candidate, usually up front, to "market" the candidate and then send the résumé to every company he or she knew who could possibly employ this candidate.

Today, that strategy has changed. Recruiters are paid by the hiring company (turn and run if a headhunter tries to charge you). Recruiters are generally categorized by the way they are paid, either with an up front retainer or after the placement is made on a contingency.

There are more than 5,000 registered recruiters. It doesn't matter how the recruiter is paid: both retained and contingency recruiters could hold your blissful dream job on their turbo-charged computer. As a general rule of thumb, retained recruiters work on more senior-level jobs (director level on up), and contingency recruiters cover the gamut, but generally work on the junior (director level on down).

I have worked on both contingency and retainer, but, for the past eight years, nearly all my work has been done on retainer (or, in rare instances, on exclusive contingency). Regardless of which recruiter type, you want a recruiter possessing strong relationships with companies that you are targeting—these are your dream companies. Usually, this means your recruiter is working on an exclusive arrangement.

You should always ask your recruiter what his or her relationship is to the company: *Are you working on retainer or contingency? Is the agreement exclusive?* If not, ask how many other recruiters are being used for the search?

Ask: *How did your relationship with this company start?* (Look for a relationship with senior management and length of time of over two years.) *How many placements have you made with this company?* (Look for more than one. You don't want to be the guinea pig.) These are important questions—to ferret out the paper-pushers from the professional recruiters.

Many companies have their own in-house recruiters. They are paid a salary and usually receive a bonus. All of their work is done for the same company, so they will probably not be looking for what's right for you; rather, they will typically try to sell you on their company as the only place you should consider. Bear this in mind when they offer you career advice. It will be obvious that their advice is myopic and biased, but that's okay. Many times, companies who have in-house recruiters still will contract third-party (that is, outside) recruiters.

Ideally, your recruiter will have an exclusive relationship with the company he or she is representing and then all you have to do is to get to the top of the pile of the recruiter's extensive list of possible candidates (more on that soon).

How to Find Recruiters

Word-of-mouth is a good starting point. Ask your network of friends and business associates if they can recommend an executive recruiter. Beyond your networking efforts, *The Directory of Executive Recruiters* by Kennedy Publications is a great resource for locating recruiters. Aptly referred to as the "red book" (it's always had a red cover,) this directory categorizes recruiters by retained (my firm is listed there) and contingency. Remember, both are acceptable and either type could potentially hold your dream job.

In the red book (found in most major bookstores and libraries and on Amazon, but consult the most recent edition—updated annually), you can search by geography and function, so you can focus your reach to recruiters who specialize in the industries you are targeting. The red book gives you the firm's name, a key contact name (usually the owner/president), phone number, email, and mailing address.

It's best to try to reach the key contact via telephone, but don't get discouraged if you don't get through; your next step is to send an email or a snail mail hard copy with a brief but professional note detailing your background and desired job and geographic preferences.

If you include a copy of your résumé, make sure you write, "Please do not present my qualifications without my prior approval" on your cover letter. This is necessary to protect yourself from headhunters (those numbskulls who earn the title headhunter) who don't have your best interests at heart. For example, some headhunters will "float" your résumé in to a company—in other words, send in your background (and claim a stake on a fee as high as 40 percent of your first year's total compensation) without you even knowing, let alone approving, the company.

This gets particularly sticky if you have targeted the company directly (on your own) and have been able to get introduced to the company (without the use of a recruiter), only to find that some headhunter has sent (floated) your résumé in to the same company—unbeknownst to you.

If the company didn't budget for a recruiter fee, this could eliminate your candidacy through no fault of your own. Be leery of the recruiter who wants your résumé without telling you about a specific opportunity including the company's name. Floaters are not helpers in your job search.

Some recruiters will take shortcuts by floating your résumé in mass quantities, hoping they'll nail an easy fee by claiming a stake on you, even if this may cost you your ideal job. Some recruiters are "aligned" with other recruiters, either with a professional network or as partners (meaning they split the fee for a candidate placement with another recruiter). You can see how your résumé can appear all over the place—quickly and without your knowledge.

Imagine you are employed and your résumé gets in the wrong hands (your boss!) and you had no idea. Don't worry. As long as you protect yourself and treat your résumé as a sacred document by being very careful about where it is sent, you are okay. When you write, "Please do not present my qualifications without my prior approval," you also protect yourself from floaters.

Do not ever post your résumé on any online service. If you must use an online service, give sketchy details about your background and don't list your identity. Recruiters search online for résumés—you could have a bounty on your head from someone you have never even met.

My intention is not to scare you from working with recruiters—there are several highly competent and honest executive recruiters, and you should reach out to them and develop a strong relationship with the ones you trust. The purpose of this chapter is to educate you on the inner workings of recruiters—the behind-the-scenes stuff you don't usually learn about—until it's too late.

The following is a sample cover letter to be sent to an executive recruiter:

Karen Peoples
21 Money St.
Mt. Laurel, NJ 08054
609.555.0200
E-Mail: karen.peoples@home.com

Ms. Mabel Bodie
Able Employment Recruitment
3400 Einstein Parkway
Princeton, NJ 08540

Dear Ms. Bodie:

If you have a client seeking a brand strategist who can deliver bottom-line results, I'd like to make a strong case for myself. My track record in business-to-business international branding and marketing has helped enhance the reputations of such firms as Chase Manhattan, The New York Stock Exchange, AT&T, and Microsoft, to name a few. I am contacting you as I believe it is time for a change. My employer is in the process of merging with another company, so I am actively exploring outside opportunities.

Of particular interest to your client firms:

I have demonstrated my strategic ability through successfully launching companies, communications departments, web sites, PR programs, ad campaigns, branding programs, and more.

I have consistently contributed my leadership skills in a corporate setting, while managing the creative process, motivating and empowering team members, fine-tuning marketing plans, and juggling multiple projects. I am a proficient top achiever and profit-minded leader.

My initiatives have resulted in increased awareness and press coverage, successful advertising campaigns, and winning branding strategies.

I am particularly interested in positions in the New York area that start at a salary range of $80K to $100K, in the following categories:

marketing partner at a venture capital firm, entailing leveraging marketing opportunities for the portfolio companies and advising them on branding and marketing strategies; brand strategist and global head of marketing for a service-oriented preferably global business; senior-management role in a mid-sized integrated agency specializing in advertising, PR, and interactive services; marketing and communications head for a high-end financial services boutique; high-end headhunter or right-hand in a large philanthropic organization.

I'd like to meet with you to discuss adding value to one of your client firms as I've done for my previous employers. *Please do not present my qualifications without my prior approval.* I'll contact you soon to arrange a meeting. Should you wish to contact me before then, I can be reached during the day on my direct line (609.555.6300) or at home most evenings (609.555.0200).

Sincerely,
Karen Peoples

Some Dos
for Dealing with a Recruiter

When you get a recruiter "live" on the phone or, even better, face-to-face in a meeting, the following advice should help you gain points with him or her:

- Treat all of your communication with a recruiter as though he or she were the hiring manager.
- Always be professional. View each interaction as if you were on an interview—it usually is. I am continually forming my opinions about a candidate each time we interact.

- Be clear and concise about your background. Recruiters can size you up quickly by your ability to verbalize your thoughts in a clear, concise manner.

- Be honest and forthright about what you want to do. What are your goals? The only way a recruiter can help you is for you to clearly describe your ideal job. If the position and/or company the recruiter is pitching to you is not right, say so, and give your reason(s) in a professional, polite manner. Sometimes, turning down a job opportunity the right way can lead to the next call when your true blissful dream job becomes available.

- Be helpful. If the position is not right for you, try to recommend someone else. This will elevate your status with any recruiter.

Some Don'ts
for Dealing with a Recruiter

- Don't call to ask, "Did you get my résumé?" If you emailed it and it is in your Sent folder, he or she received it.

- Don't ask a recruiter to do your résumé for you. Your résumé needs to be impressive on its own. Let the recruiter offer you advice on how to enhance your résumé to tailor it to the dream company's hot buttons. Graciously accept his or her advice, and if you agree, integrate it into your résumé.

- Don't overstay your welcome. Be mindful that recruiters are on the phone all day long with a stack of calls to make. Speaking "live" with a recruiter is a fairly rare occurrence. You gain points by being concise and direct.

- Don't call him or her *headhunter* even if he or she does. Always call him or her an *executive recruiter* (or, in my case, Mystic Career Guide and Life Coach ... just wanted to see if you are paying attention).
- Don't expect a recruiter to tell you about more than one job that matches your background. They will usually try to sell you on the one that is the easiest fit for them or the most pressing at the time, even if it's not the best fit for you.
- Don't lie about previous employers, salary history, or education degrees. Ever!
- Don't call recruiters too often. Touching base once a month is usually about right. Weekly (and, especially, daily) calls become annoying and are usually screened and eventually ignored.

A good recruiter will stay in touch with you from time to time, especially if he or she has graded you an "A player" (topnotch candidate). My firm uses a subjective grading system in order like grades in school (A, A-, B+, B, B-, C+, and C). Following the advice you've just read should help you earn an "A." "C" players don't land ideal jobs and aren't in my database.

How Can I Get on the "A" List?

The following tips will help:

- Be organized. Have good, clear, and concise thoughts and questions. Treat the recruiter as if he or she were the hiring manager. In some cases, they are.
- Be available. Recruiters (myself included) usually work at warp speed—making hundreds of calls in a given day. A recruiter's

perception of time is equivalent to dog years. Be responsive: return a recruiter's phone call as soon as possible—even if it's to say you cannot talk until later, and schedule a time and date when you both will be available. Failure to return a call within twenty-four hours says, "I'm not interested."

- Do the research. Check out the company online, talk to customers, network—do everything you can to show that you are truly interested in the opportunity.

- Ask good questions. Do your own research and prepare good questions. Asking the recruiter pertinent and well-thought-out questions gives the recruiter confidence you will do well on an interview (remember, you are treating the recruiter as if he or she were the hiring manager).

- Be professional. If the recruiter is not professional (and many do give the profession a well-earned bad name), don't be unprofessional yourself.

- Be honest. If you have already taken another job, say so. Express thanks to the recruiter for thinking of you, but be direct and forthright.

- Be helpful. If you are not interested in the job the recruiter is selling, say so, and give your honest reasons, but always try to give recommendations of people you think could do the job. Being a good source elevates your "grade," and you are more likely to get the call on a better job next time.

- Set up a network. For the "good" recruiter you meet, stay in contact with him or her. Develop and foster a strong relationship. Try establishing your own personal network of recruiters you know and trust. There are a handful of candidates who have stayed in contact with me for over fifteen years—I just placed one in a dream job.

If a recruiter has a job with an interesting company that sounds exciting to you, and says he or she would like to "present you" (in other words,
the recruiter will email your résumé with a brief cover note to his or her
client), express enthusiasm, and ask as many questions as you can. Most
recruiters know their client well both personally and professionally (I
consider my clients my friends) and can give you pertinent information
to integrate into your résumé and interview strategy.

Look for things beyond what you can find on the company website or
in the annual report. Ask for the following information:

- Background on the hiring manager (personal and
  professional). Marital status, children, religion, educational
  background, hometown, and hobbies.
- Reason for the opening. You want to hear that it's due to
  promotion or ideally a newly created position. If the previous
  person was terminated, ask why. If terminated, ask how long
  was he or she in the position?
- Hot buttons for the company and the hiring manager. What
  are the most pressing problems they are looking to solve?
- Ideal candidate profile—which attributes are most important
  to the hiring manager.
- Key challenges for the job.
- Salary range, including bonus potential and actual payout,
  benefit information, and perks.
- Company history. When and how did it start? Is it family-
  owned, private, or publicly traded?

Treating your recruiter with respect and demonstrating strong
interpersonal skills will pay dividends and move you closer to your
ideal job. I have many "A" candidates whom I have placed more than
once and who always hear about the best jobs I am working on. Use this
advice and forge some strong relationships. Put your strong recruiter
network to work for you.

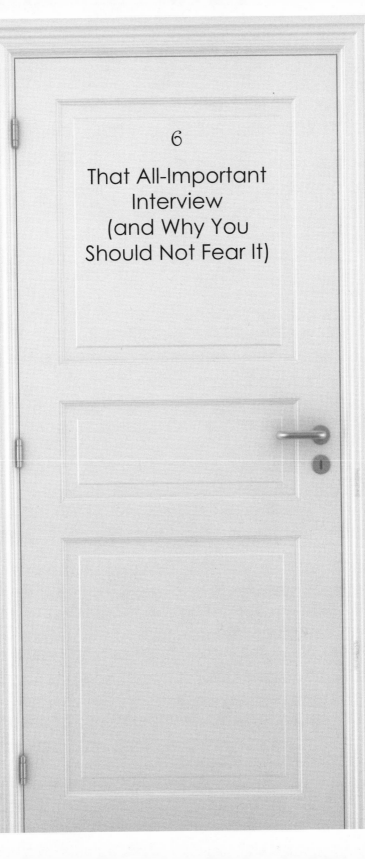

6

That All-Important Interview (and Why You Should Not Fear It)

Not so fast. Let's start long before the interview. I'll call this phase the pre-interview. Because the more prepared for the interview you are, the more likely you will get that blissful dream job. Here are three things you need to do:

- Prepare
- Prepare
- Prepare

Get the picture? You cannot over-prepare for an interview. You need to know as much as you can about the prospective company, its culture, its history, and the challenges, which you will be asked to help solve. Also you need to know as much as possible about the position for which you are interviewing: why it is open, the background of the person you would report to—plus likes/dislikes, hot buttons, and management style. I know I am being redundant here, but preparation is the gateway to success.

An executive recruiter should know all of this information and should be more than willing to share it with you; the better prepared you are and the better you do in the interview, the better the recruiter looks in the client's eyes. You are on the same page as the recruiter; view him or her as your ally. Ask for as much pertinent information as you can.

If you're not using a recruiter, it will be more difficult (but not impossible) to obtain all this helpful information. Beyond the plethora of information available online today, do some networking. Start by contacting some of the company's customers. Go to their business place and gather as much information as you can. Do some mystery shopping and ask questions of as many people as you can.

Interview Snafus to Avoid Like the Plague

As you prepare yourself for the interview (this includes your contact with your recruiter), there are some attitudinal snafus that may derail your interview—even before you have it. These will be a mini-lesson in the concept of contrast, so think of the polar opposite of how to act, These points should go without saying, but you'd be shocked at how many times a candidate commits these blunders:

- Not asking any questions
- Condemning your past employers or bosses
- Being unable to take criticism
- Having poor personal appearance
- Being cynical, lazy, and indecisive
- Being a poor listener, overbearing, and a "know it all"
- Arriving late

- Maintaining poor eye contact
- Being unable to express yourself clearly
- Expressing overemphasis on money

So let's spend some time addressing these situations so you can avoid them.

Attire

Dress codes at companies vary widely these days. But the proper attire for an interview hasn't changed.

As a rule of thumb, always dress your best for the interview. You are probably saying, "C'mon, I know how to dress." How you dress everyday and how you dress for an interview are two entirely different animals. Even if the company is business casual, men should dress in a conservative suit and tie, and women should wear a conservative suit. Women should look polished but not overdone (minimal jewelry, makeup, and heels that aren't too high).

Navy blue is the best option. Shoes need to be nicely polished and look as if they are brand new. Have your shirts or blouses professionally laundered or choose shirts made of wrinkle-resistant fabric. Have a friend (or a mirror) give you a once-over before you go to the interview. I heard a story of a candidate who waltzed into an interview with toilet paper hanging off the back of his shoe—like a streamer on a float in a parade. He paraded himself out of the job and didn't even realize it.

Your physical impressions get you hired so don't underestimate the power of wearing the proper attire.

Visualization

This may be the most important way to prepare yourself prior to your interview. If you have been practicing and becoming proficient at meditating (explained earlier), great. If not, you can still visualize. Numerous world-class athletes visualize for success: Tiger Woods, Michael Phelps, Lance Armstrong, and Michael Jordan are a few.

Why is visualization—which has been scientifically proven to greatly enhance performance and is used widely in athletic competition by the best in the world—rarely used in business? Laziness?

When you learn you have an upcoming interview, spend about fifteen minutes before you go to bed and practice visualizing. Close your eyes and see yourself in the actual interview. Give yourself sample questions (you can use questions from an upcoming chapter and add your own) and then answer them in your mind. Feel great as you give perfect answers. See the interviewer smile with his or her approval. Feel the connection with the interviewer.

The day of the interview, arrive one-half-hour early and find a private place (your car or even the bathroom, if needed) and mentally review all the points you want to make with your interviewer. Mentally give yourself some positive affirmations such as, "I'm going to have a great interview; I'm prepared for any question and confident I'm the right person for the job." "This is my dream job."

The practice of visualization is paramount to success in an interview. Meditating—relaxing your mind—just prior to the interview will quell your natural nervousness, allowing you to channel your energy into a productive, positive interview.

When Tiger Woods is preparing to putt, do you think he is thinking anything other than, "I can make the putt?" No! And, usually, he sinks it. The more positive your thoughts are before, during, and after the interview, the more likely you are to nail it.

Three-Scenes Technique

Consistent with the message of this book—mystical plus practical—this section will combine meditation with a practical application. I will provide you with a very powerful application of visualization. Perform this technique while in the meditative state of alpha. By now, you are probably getting more proficient at meditating, and it will come easily to you. This exercise will take only about fifteen minutes.

With eyes closed, move your eyes as if you were looking slightly upward (about 20 degrees) and picture yourself on your mental screen. Spend about two minutes visualizing yourself right now. See the sights, hear the sounds, feel the feeling all around you. As you begin feeling comfortable, move the image to your right with your eyes and pull the next image of yourself from your left onto your screen in front of you. This will be you in the actual interview. See yourself answering questions with confidence. The questions and answers you are asked are flowing—you have rehearsed and rehearsed (like riding a bicycle). See the interviewer smiling at your answers. Feel the connection. You know you are nailing it. You are well on your way to getting that dream job offer. Hold on to the visualization for about five minutes.

Afterward, again push the screen to the right with your eyes (past) and pull the third visualization from your left (future) onto your center screen (present). This will be you in the job six months from your start date. See yourself doing the job and really enjoying it. Really hone in on the good feeling of being in your blissful dream job—enjoying your work, being recognized for jobs well done, building meaningful relationships with everyone you come in contact with. Be as vivid as you can—the more realistic you can make it, the better. Try to hold this visualization for at least five minutes. When you are ready to finish, feel the gratitude for having your ideal job.

This is one of the most powerful techniques of visualization, and it has been widely used with astounding results.

Einstein believed there was no time reality. Though it's hard to fathom this concept as you watch a clock ticking away, he has been proven right. He was referring to the progressively relaxed states of consciousness: alpha, theta, and delta. In alpha—during which you are still conscious but relaxed (ten BPS—beats per second of your brain waves). There is no time dimension. The past is to your right, the present is in front of you, and the future is to your left. This three-scenes technique creates your own reality (devoid of time limitations) by using the Law of Attraction.

The stronger and more realistic your thoughts and feelings, the more likely your visualization will manifest into reality.

How to Relax before the Interview

We just covered mental preparation prior to an interview. Now, it's time to discuss techniques to relax your body. The application will give you practical results. Remember, you are all energy and vibrate at differing rates from everything else in the universe.

I have read a lot about alternative medicines: chakras, meridians, and acupuncture. If this sounds like Chinese to you, it is! The ancient Chinese, among others, developed amazing techniques to help human beings with their energy flow. Alternative medicine, long disregarded in the U.S. as voodoo medicine, is flourishing today. It's hard to drive for very long and not see a chiropractor's office. There may even be as many chiropractors' offices as McDonald's—now, that's progress.

Rather than give you zillions of things to do and get into the theories behind all this stuff, I'll give you three very simple techniques you can use to overcome nervousness about an upcoming job interview. These will help you release stress and enable your energy to flow optimally— much better than a cup of coffee (drug). All three exercises take only about five minutes total and don't require any heavy lifting. They are called

- K-27s
- Wayne Cook Posture
- Cross Crawl

K-27s

Certain points on your body, when tapped or massaged with your fingers, will positively impact your energy field, sending electrochemical impulses to your brain and releasing neurotransmitters (feel-good chemicals). By tapping and/or massaging three specific points on your body, you can activate a sequence of responses that will restore you when you are tired, increase your vitality, and even strengthen your immune system amid stress (so you won't get sick before or after the interview).

Figure 1: K-27 Tap

1. Simply place your fingers on your collarbone and slide them inward toward the center and find the bumps where they stop. Drop about an inch beneath these corners and slightly outward to the K-27s (see Figure 1). Most people have a slight indent here that their fingers will drop into.

2. With the fingers of both your hands turned toward your body, cross your hands over one another, with the middle finger of each hand now resting on the opposite K-27 point. Crossing your hands is important because it assists the energy to cross over from the left brain hemisphere to the right side of the body and vice versa—left hemisphere to right side.

3. Tap and/or massage the points firmly while breathing deeply—in through your nose and out through your mouth. Continue for about thirty seconds.

4. After you have tapped/massaged your K-27s, you can boost the effect by hooking the middle finger of one hand in your navel and resting the fingers of your other hand on the K-27 points. With as many fingers as you can hook into your navel, pull upward for two or three deep breaths. You will likely feel a stretch below your belly.

Do this right before your interview. Tapping your K-27s (chakra points) has been proven to help you think more clearly and give you a burst of energy. An interesting side note: Next time you go to a zoo, visit the gorilla cages. If they are active, notice that gorillas will thump their chest and hit their K-27s with their fists before a confrontation with another gorilla. Now, I'm pretty sure that these gorillas didn't read this book, yet they instinctively know how to pump up their energy before a fight—by thumping their K-27s. Smart apes!

Wayne Cook Posture

Named to honor Wayne Cook, a pioneering researcher of bioenergetic force fields, this is a basic technique to literally move stress hormones out of your body. Almost immediately, you will feel better, be able to think more clearly, and see with greater perspective. It takes only about two minutes to do the Wayne Cook Posture:

Figure 2. Wayne Cook Posture

1. Sit in a chair with your spine straight. Place your right foot over your left knee. Wrap your left hand around your right ankle and your right hand around the ball of your right foot (see Figure 2).

2. Breathe in slowly through your nose, allowing your breath to lift your body as you breathe in. At the same time, pull your leg toward you, creating a stretch. As you exhale, breathe out of your mouth slowly, and feel your body relax. Repeat this slow breathing and stretching four or five times.

3. Switch to the other foot. Place your left foot over your right knee. Wrap your right hand around your left ankle and your left hand around the ball of your left foot. Use the same breathing.

4. Uncross your legs and place your fingertips together forming a pyramid. Bring your thumbs to rest on your "third eye," just above the bridge of your nose and between your eyes. Breathe slowly in through your nose. Then breathe out through your mouth, allowing your thumbs to separate slowly across your forehead, pulling the skin.

5. Bring your thumbs back to the third eye position. Slowly bring your hands down in front of you, pulling them together into a prayerful position while breathing deeply. Surrender into your own breathing.

Wayne Cook was successful in treating dyslexia and stuttering. This procedure connects the energy circuitry in a manner that allows a smooth flow throughout your body. Stress short-circuits your forebrain (thinking brain). This simple technique will help you communicate clearly and focus well.

Cross Crawl

This simple exercise will facilitate the crossover of energy between the brain's right and left hemispheres. You will feel more balanced, think more clearly, improve your coordination (nothing worse than tripping and falling into the interviewer's desk), and harmonize your energies.

Prior to starting the Cross Crawl, tap your K-27s again to ensure that your energies are traveling in their natural direction. The Cross Crawl is very easy to do; it's like marching in place and only takes about a minute:

Figure 3: The Cross Crawl

1. While standing, lift your right arm and left leg simultaneously (see Figure 3).
2. As you let them down, raise your left arm and right leg.

3. Repeat, this time exaggerating the lift of your leg and the swing of your arm across the midline to the opposite side of your body.

4. Continue in this exaggerated march for at least a minute while breathing deeply in through your nose and out through your mouth.

The effectiveness of the Cross Crawl is based primarily on the fact that the left hemisphere of your brain needs to send information to the right side of your body, and vice versa. If energy from the left or right hemisphere is not adequately crossing over to the opposite side of your body, you cannot access and utilize your brain's full capacity or your body's full intelligence. This basic exercise will energize you.

Showtime! The Interview

Okay, you are mentally, physically, and emotionally prepared: it's showtime! The big event!

The actual interview itself usually lasts for only an hour. It should help you relax just to realize that one hour will fly by. Bear in mind, there is equal pressure on the interviewer as there is on you, the interviewee.

There is a myth in American business that once a person is promoted to management, he or she becomes magically endowed with all the necessary management skills. Very few people in "management" have been adequately taught to interview (another course that should be offered in schools but isn't). Most junior interviewers just stumble through interviewing and learn from trial and error.

I can still remember conducting my first interview; the term *shaky* is an understatement, but with time and practice, I became proficient in interviewing. You will get a quick sense of the experience level of your interviewer: skilled—savvy in systematic techniques for ferreting out your past and a good evaluator of your skills from effective Q&As; or bumbling—he or she may even have trouble phrasing questions adequately. Both are equally challenging when it comes to winning an offer. The advice you will receive will help you with all types of interviewers.

Beyond the all-important first impression, there are four sections to the interview. The more prepared you are for each section, the more likely the interview will produce an offer. The following are the four major sections of the interview:

- The introduction
- Your background
- Information about the company
- Closing (discussed in detail in chapter 7)

The Introduction

If you feel a little nervous, congratulate yourself, you are a human being. You are, after all, interviewing for your ideal job. The more you are able to channel your nervous energy into an amazing performance, the more likely you are to receive an offer. Tell yourself you're ready and take some relaxing deep breaths. The introduction is the easy part.

A firm handshake while smiling and smoothly introducing yourself is the most important element toward making a strong first impression. Many interviewers say, "I make my mind up about a candidate in the first five seconds." Do not underestimate this vital step. If your nerves have given you a clammy, wet hand, wipe it off right before the handshake. If your hand is cold, warm it up—run hot water in the bathroom if necessary. The firm handshake has to leave a favorable impression.

After the initial greeting, follow the interviewer's lead on where to sit and remember to keep your posture upright. Your posture should reflect confidence and professionalism—a comfortable readiness.

Allow the interviewer to "break the ice," usually by picking a light topic: the weather, the surroundings, a current event. Again, follow the interviewer's lead and ease into the interview with grace.

How well you handle this first five minutes usually determines whether or not the interviewer feels comfortable with you (and vice versa). You'll know when the introduction section is over because the interviewer will transition from small talk to an introductory question.

Your Background

An astute interviewer will usually try to get you to talk about 80 percent of the time by asking open-ended questions like these:

- *Tell me about yourself?*
- *What brings you here today?*
- *First, I'd like you to walk me through your background.*

I will give you great sample answers to these open-ended questions and many others in the next chapter.

The Two Most Important Questions

Keep in mind, there is pressure on the interviewer. It is a difficult task to get to know you in the confines of an hour or less. There are two critical questions in the back of the interviewer's mind:

- *Why do you want to leave your current company?*
- *Why do you want to work for us?*

The *Why do you want to leave your current company?* question is a potential landmine. Don't step on the landmine. The answer needs to be brief and well-prepared. Less is more here. Many interviewees open up Pandora's Box at this point, thinking that brutal honesty is what's needed now—as a way to bond with the interviewer. Don't let your guard down.

The interviewer actually doesn't want to hear about all the evil things your boss has done to you in the past, or all the broken promises, or all the times you were overlooked for a promotion, or screwed out of a bonus, or how bad the training is, or how horrible the culture is. In fact, usually, the interviewer is wincing inside as this question is asked, hoping you don't commit interview suicide by stepping on that landmine.

So, what's the best answer? If you are using an executive search firm, tell the interviewer you weren't looking, that things have been going well, and that the recruiter kept persisting and, after looking at the opportunity, you agreed it would be a great job and company. Perfect. You have remained positive, upbeat, and even confident, without smearing your previous company.

If the company was not using a search firm, use the "I wasn't really looking—I'm happy here, but this opportunity seemed like a dream job. I've always wanted to work for this company, and customer X and Y and Z have spoken highly about your company."

Another possible answer is, "Well as you've probably seen in *The Wall Street Journal,* our company is being divested and though I have enjoyed my work, there is uncertainty about our future." The interviewer will usually nod in agreement even if he or she doesn't read *The Wall Street Journal*—just being able to quote the business bible is impressive and also shows you know how to read.

The quicker you get to the next question, *Why do you want to work for us?* the better. In this important step, you win the job or lose it. In an interview, it's usually not the most qualified person—on paper—who gets the job; it's the person who goes in to get a job versus merely to have a job interview.

That deserves repeating: it's the person who goes in to get a job who wins the offer; merely showing up for an interview doesn't cut it. Enthusiasm toward the company, the job, and the opportunity can make all the difference in the world.

Prepare your answer. It needs to be brief, positive, genuine, and enthusiastic. Say, "I have always wanted to work for this company and this job seems ideal for my background." Tell the interviewer what you can bring to the table by using examples of your experiences.

Brag Book

The brag book is a very important item to bring to the interview. Many times, an interviewer will ask you to describe your accomplishments, successes, desirable personality traits, and so on. It is very effective to have this information in print form as a leave-behind and as a talking point during the interview. Your brag book should contain this information:

- A clean cotton-bound copy of your résumé
- Performance appraisals
- Examples of your work, particularly ones that were successful and would be important to the interviewer
- Letters of recommendation
- Copies of awards you have won

Place this information in a binder or folder and hand it to the interviewer as quickly as possible. A brag book gives the impression that you are professional, want the job badly enough to take the time to put it together, and takes the BS factor out of verbal-only answers.

What is the BS factor? Anyone can BS their way through an interview, but a written leave-behind is much more believable. It's one thing to say, "I'm persistent, a team player, and a high achiever," and an entirely different—and more effective technique—to show it with what bosses actually wrote about you and with examples of your work. A sample of your work shows the work and is instantly both impressive and believable.

Finally, your brag book is a way to differentiate yourself from the others after the interviews have ended. The interviewer is likely to read through it after your one-hour interview has ended. In essence, you are able to sell yourself even after you have gone; your brag book can sway the decision your way without your having to say a word; it's all been said by those who have observed your work.

In addition, the brag book makes an interviewer less apt to feel the need to obtain references on you—something that can backfire if the wrong person is contacted—unbeknownst to you (we all have a few enemies; it's no coincidence that the word *enemy* is similar to *envy*).

Remember, it's not always the most qualified person for the job who gets the job. The person who wants the job the most, gets the job. The brag book shows you want the job.

Information about the Company

By now, you have either won the job—which you will feel—or the interviewer has kept his or her nonverbal signals hidden. This is the homestretch. A little previous preparation and improvisation will keep the momentum building in your favor.

Usually the interviewer will shift into asking you, "Do you have any questions for me?" An enthusiastic yes is required; answering no can drop you out of the running. Prepare a list of questions for this interaction. It is very common to blank out at this point, so having a notebook/sheet of paper right there in front of you will help greatly.

Try to prioritize your questions using the "put yourself in the interviewer's shoes" mode. This is your opportunity to shine (pun intended)—showing you have done your research. You should ask "kiss up" questions—incorporating genuine positives about the company into your questions. For example:

- *Everyone I've talked to—customers, competitors, and even former employees—say that your company is a great place to work. What do you think makes it tick?*

- *Your financial results have been impressive and at the top of the industry. Where do you think this company will be in five years?*
- *I've been very impressed with your latest new product/ service. What do you think has been your company's greatest achievement?*

The trick with these questions is to connect with your interviewer's perspective. This is imperative. Avoid asking critical questions (the Nuremberg approach) that put the interviewer on the defensive. Do not ask any negative questions about the results or the culture of the company. Verboten: if the company is coming off a lousy year, don't turn on the bright lights and pick a scab. Conversely, if you can get the interviewer to feel good about your questions, you have probably sealed the deal at this point.

7

Tell me about yourself and Other Dreaded Interview Questions (with Ace-in-the-Hole Answers)

At some point, the interviewer takes over and starts asking you a whole litany of questions. Many interviewers bring prepared questions. Several undisciplined candidates experience fear at this phase of the interview. Fear is rooted in lack of confidence in the future. Think about it. Fear is nothing more than an irrational lack of focus on the present.

It is important for you to be confident, focused, and in the present moment, for the interview. The purpose of this section is to give you the confidence that you can answer any question. The following are sample interview questions, taken from actual interviews—with recommended answers:

Q:
Tell me about yourself.

This is possibly the most common interview question. First, ask a qualifier: "Are you interested in my business or personal life?" Then, put yourself in the interviewer's shoes for your answer. Be prepared for "both" as the answer. Intersperse as many of the following traits as you can into your answer:

Personal Traits

- Enthusiastic: Many interviewers expect you to entertain them. The more engaged you are with genuine energy and enthusiasm, the more likely you are to win the job offer. Your enthusiasm is contagious.

- Positive: You see the glass as full every time. There is always upside potential.

- Initiative: You set very lofty goals for yourself (have examples in mind) and strive to accomplish your goals through action.

- Determined: Paint yourself as a winner despite all obstacles and that you embrace new challenges.

- Confident: There's a fine line between seeming *cocky* and being *confident*. I'd like you to break out the brag book here with some previous performance appraisals and highlight your positive traits through what your previous supervisors wrote about you.

- Concise thinker: Do not let yourself ramble on during this or any other answer.

- Communicator: Your ability to verbalize your thoughts and write effective emails and proposals are important to any company.

Business Traits

- Integrity: The cornerstone to any effective relationship. You always treat decisions as if you owned the company yourself. You follow the motto: "Do what's right."
- Efficient: By setting your goals and efficiently managing your time, you get the job done right—and quickly.
- Reliable: You are always counted on, and trusted, to get any task done and done right.
- Analytical: You make educated decisions based on facts and weigh the pros and cons carefully.
- Proud: You do only work that makes you proud and again—referring to your brag book/performance appraisal(s)—that makes your supervisors proud.
- Personable: You are a good listener, but can verbalize your thoughts in a concise, cohesive manner to best communicate any subject.
- Problem Solving: You are a problem-solver who can run the business.

Try to be concise in your answer and tailor it to the needs of the position and the company. Practice your response as often as you can.

Q:
What are your three greatest strengths and three greatest weaknesses?

This is a very common interview question. The first part is a slam dunk; the second is a potential landmine unless you are careful. For strengths, keep in mind that every company needs people who can do three things well: (1) earn revenue, (2) save money, and (3) save time. Plug this in, interspersed with some business traits and make the interviewer smile.

For weaknesses, don't ingest truth serum and tell of your paranoid fantasy to kill your current boss. Avoid admitting to character flaws like the plague. I prefer a "weakness" to be skill-related and past tense: "I wasn't astute with PowerPoint when I first started, but I read a great book, practiced, and became very proficient; now I train others in PowerPoint presentations."

You are admitting to something that everyone had trouble with at first. You are not born with computer software skills, so this is not a damaging answer; furthermore, you can show that you are a quick study, able to learn it and then teach it. Any time you can demonstrate how you overcame a weakness, all the better.

Another good "weakness" example is to give a general answer in which you can plug perceived strengths: "I am passionate about my work and always give each task my all. So, when sometimes I see others loafing, I can get frustrated. I have improved by always trying to demonstrate a positive attitude and hope it will catch on," or "I set lofty goals for myself and am sometimes too demanding of myself."

Again, you have another chance to mention that you are a goal-setter who raises the bar very high. Not a bad weakness. The trick with discussing your weaknesses is to avoid the landmine answer. Turn your weakness into an actual strength with a throw-away, past-tense skill that you have now learned.

———

Q:
What keeps you up at night?

Another landmine that you cannot step on. This is another way of asking for weaknesses. As you begin to feel more and more comfortable with the interviewer, there is a tendency to let your guard down. Don't! The answer is: "I work so hard that I rarely have a difficult time sleeping. I believe in proper time management and recharging my batteries with sound sleep."

Q:
Tell me how you moved up
through your last company.

A good question particularly if he or she is looking for a promotable candidate—and aren't they all? Here you can intersperse more about your personal and business traits. Be very complimentary of the company you work for: "The training was superb" or "I was fortunate to have had some great mentors who really helped me." It will be hard not to ramble a little, but focus on the promotions by title as a result of dedicated hard work and outstanding accomplishments with downright genius.

Q:
How would your boss describe you?

You can immediately point to the brag book packet you handed over during the interview, which contained a fresh copy of your résumé printed on 100% cotton, watermarked paper (usually called "résumé paper" at retailers like Target, OfficeMax, and Office Depot), previous performance appraisals, examples of your work, and letters of recommendation. This show-and-tell gives you greater credibility in the eyes of the interviewer. It can be very powerful to point out that your boss wrote, "Joe Schmoe is a top performer, dedicated, takes tremendous pride in his work, and sets demanding goals for himself. I have learned from him."

Q:
How would your spouse describe you?

This one can be tricky if you are going through a bitter divorce. Even if you are—and it's none of the interviewer's business—the answer is always an upbeat, positive response: "Loving, generous, supportive, inspirational, fun to be around, and a great role-model for our kids."

Q:

If you could be a color, which one would you be?

I was actually asked this question by an impressive, Ivy-League–educated, African-American female in a high-powered job interview. Talk about a landmine question for a Caucasian male! If I answered "black," I would have been seen as kissing up to her, and disingenuous; if I answered "white," I would seem like a member of the Klan.

I smiled and answered: "The rainbow." She smiled, looked interested and asked, "Why?" I replied, "There are four basic personality types in individuals, and I pride myself on trying to recognize and adapt to each one, depending on the situation. Sometimes I need to be red; sometimes green; sometimes black and white; sometimes even pink."

She laughed and actually said, "Great answer!"

Q:

If you could be an animal, which one would you be?

I was asked this as the follow up to the color question. My instinct told me to avoid saying panther and polar bear—no benefit in messing up my previous answer with the black and white thing. Also, shark, snake, and turtle were landmine replies.

I answered, "Jaguar." She looked intrigued, smiled, and asked, "Why?"

I replied, "The jaguar is very versatile—able to patiently wait for its prey for hours on end if needed and can pounce with lightning speed and grace. Plus, it's a cool car!"

She smiled and said, "Great answer" for the second time as she reached into her purse to pull out her car keys with the Jaguar emblem on it (I got the job offer).

Q:
How long would you stay with our company?

This is a good question to get asked; it is a "buy" signal, implying he or she is thinking of offering you a job. This one is tricky though—*is he or she concerned that I would leave after a short while?*

Don't take the bait. Put the hot potato back in the interviewer's lap with: "I would hope to have a great career with this company. I respond well to direction and am always looking to learn. I define success as being ready when an opportunity arises. How long do you think I'd be challenged here?" Back in his or her lap. Touché!

Q:
Describe how you do a major project.

This is a perfect opportunity to demonstrate that you are a business manager who can identify and solve problems: "I believe in effective strategic planning that involves both forward thinking (in other words, what resources will I need?) and backward thinking (for example, if the deadline is the end of the quarter, what steps need to be made and at what time to achieve a successful outcome?)."

Q:
How do you handle stress?

This is tricky; the interviewer implies you get stressed out. Does the interviewer mean personal stress or business stress inherent to business cycles?

The best way to answer this is to deflect it, "I avoid stress by careful time management. There are only so many hours in a given day, so I try to maximize my time by setting effective goals. On the personal side, I exercise regularly, eat right, and get adequate sleep—I think this alleviates stress."

Q:
What would you do during your first ninety days on the job?

Fair question in the interviewer's mind but unfair to the interviewee. The interviewer cannot expect you to know the intricacies of the position and the company, so you can be general here.

After responding with some generalities, I like to send this one back to the interviewer. "I believe in setting my goals in line with the company's near-term objectives, which I would expect to receive right away. Then I would prioritize my time relative to achieving those goals. What are the company's most pressing needs right now and do you offer a standard training program?"

Q:
Are you open to relocation?

Hopefully, prior to the interview, you were able to find out where the position is located—out of your home office (as is becoming more accepted), in a branch office, or inside the corporate headquarters. A qualifier is needed here so you don't step on a landmine, "It's my understanding that this job would be out of my home office. Is that right?"

If the answer is a "yes but," find out where the hiring manager wants you located and answer accordingly. Keep in mind, your objective in the interview is to get the job offer first; then you can decide. If, unbeknownst to you, they want to move you to Nowheresville, Kentucky, you can always say no.

Don't take yourself out of the running now. If the question is, "Would you move for a promotion?" the answer is, "I would consider relocation for the right opportunity to grow with the company." Even if your sick, live-in, mother-in-law is in your basement and your spouse would crucify you for even considering relocation, don't step on the landmine by answering no.

After you are with a company and have proven yourself to be a valuable employee, many times there is flexibility on location. Make sure your answer keeps you in the running.

Q:
What experience do you have for this job?

This is a key question in the back of the mind of the interviewer but unfortunately, without proper background information, you should not answer blindly. It is proper to ask a qualifier such as, "What are some of the problems facing the company currently, and what projects will I be involved in?" Only by asking this qualifier will you identify the priorities of your future boss.

The interviewer will think favorably of your thought process with this qualifier. The interviewer's answer will give you enough ammo so you can adequately answer the question. Use your brag book if you can show examples of your having accomplished like tasks and solving similar problems. The more you show yourself as a problem-solver who can run the business, the better.

Q:
What do you like and dislike about your current job?

This is what I call the "wince question"—the interviewer winces just after asking it, hoping you don't step on a landmine by blurting out a negative answer.

This takes you back to, "Why do you want to leave your current company?" Don't take the bait. Even if your current company is a torture chamber, don't tell the interviewer. He or she is actually looking for you to give a positive response and not rant and rave about your current job and company.

Focus on the positives. Say, "As you know, I wasn't looking and am doing well in my current job. I love the training and the culture. Our products and services are superb. My boss is supportive and a great teacher. But my company is being sold, so I'm concerned about future security. Regardless of my company's security, both this opportunity and your company seem ideal to me."

Be upbeat about all your experiences and shift gears to show how applicable your training is to the job for which you are interviewing. It may be a good time to point to your brag book if you have an example of applicable work that was exemplary. Use the comment, "As you know, I wasn't actively looking ... but, the more I looked into this company and this position, the more interested I became."

The interviewer by now has probably given you some information about what's important. Hit 'em with his or her own "hot buttons" here.

Q:
What parts of your job do you consider most important?

Caution: exercise care. A flippant answer can derail your progress and end the interview fast. Think "big picture" in your answer—minutia will send you packing. Again, paint yourself as someone who is a business manager who can run the business. Stress your ability to manage your time wisely and prioritize. You are someone who sets lofty, effective goals and accomplishes them.

Q:
How do you feel about working overtime?

Now's not the time to tell the interviewer how you cannot work any extra hours because you are training for the Iron Man Triathlon and have a sick parent and see a shrink five times per week for your paranoid fantasy about killing your boss. The best answer is, "Though I pride myself on time-management and prioritization skills, I realize that extra time is sometimes needed."

Q:
What are you hoping to gain from this job?

Make sure you know the challenges of the job that are important to the interviewer (remember, put yourself in his or her shoes). If not, ask a qualifier to discover the challenges. With this ammo, you have a loaded gun and can shoot back with examples of how you have applicable experience.

Point to the brag book if you can. Unload some more ideal personal and business traits here. Convince the interviewer that you are ready to tackle the challenges immediately. The more the interviewer has confidence that you can do it, the more likely you will obtain the offer.

Q:

Your experience is not in our industry. Do you think you can succeed in a different industry?

This one is comical in a way. Every employer feels that what they do is the most complicated and difficult thing imaginable. The truth of the matter is, everything can be learned with proper fundamentals. Emphasize those of your fundamentals that are universally desired. Draw from your ideal personal and business traits.

If this issue really were a knockout punch for your candidacy, then you wouldn't be given an interview in the first place. Don't cower; display confidence that you are a quick study with a demonstrated track record of success.

Q:

Have you ever been terminated from your job?

If you haven't, this is an easy answer, "No, and I don't plan on it happening anytime soon!"

This is a very tricky response if you have. It's really none of the interviewer's business anyway, but an unqualified yes opens up Pandora's Box, taking up the better part of the valuable and limited remaining interview time.

In my career, every company I joined either sold outright or the division I was in was put on the chopping blocks. The 1980s might have produced some cool music—and hair bands—but in business, it was nearly impossible to avoid going through corporate mergers and acquisitions, downsizings, rightsizings, cutbacks, layoffs, workforce reductions, bankruptcies, and closings (dot-com people please stand up). If anything, the period produced more creative ways for employers to say, "You're fired!"

If you were part of a job loss due to a dot-bomb not making it, it's not going to do you any harm to be "let go." Same with acquisitions (the acquirer is usually the conqueror). But if you were terminated for cause or any other performance reason, and there is a gap on your résumé, be prepared with a concise, convincing answer like, "While at Company XYZ, as you may know, we went through a number of department closings and downsizings. The department I was in was affected, and I was offered an early-retirement package. I took it and spent the time exploring all my options and patiently looking for the right job. The generous financial package allowed me to be patient so I didn't have to jump at the first offer that I received."

End by flipping it back in the interviewer's lap with, "What is the likelihood of a downsizing in this company?"

Q:
Describe a challenging time when others relied on you to interpret information for them.

The interviewer is looking for you to use knowledge of the source to communicate in an understandable way. Avoid merely restating what was communicated with little adaptation around the recipient's needs.

A possible answer is, "I was a member of a seven-person, multi-functional task force. Our challenge was to come up with a solution for a problem we were having on one of our production lines. There was some technical data that seemed like ancient hieroglyphics to everyone, but I was able to disseminate it into a usable, recommended solution.

I pride myself on using all of the information available, and making it practical—in understandable language."

Q:
Describe your most effective speech.

If you have ever had any training in speech and communication, interject it now; it shows you are a professional who is properly trained.

I attended Executive Techniques, a two-day training seminar during which each participant critiqued the other presentations. It provided very useful feedback and helped me improve my presentation skills immensely.

Many schools offer courses in public speaking; mention your experience if you can. If you haven't had any professional training or courses, describe your planning and mastery of the subject ahead of time, and use of visuals (PowerPoint knowledge is a benefit to most employers) and your overall presentation techniques.

Avoid talking about your phobia of public speaking and the fact that you have a persistent incontinence problem when you are put on the spot in front of a group of people.

Q:

Tell me about a time when you had to communicate under difficult circumstances.

This is similar to the "interpret information" question just discussed—only this one focuses on your communication skills.

Speak to your preparation and mastery of the content and that you had a good understanding of the problem from carefully listening. The perception of a presentation is that it is 90 percent talking, but you believe that the most effective communication stems from 90 percent listening and 10 percent talking. After you fully understood the problem, you focused on the problem and did not personalize it (in other words, you didn't let egos get in the way). Say that your direct answer, which focused on the solution, was well-received and appreciated. Don't stray into any negative feelings you may have had—focus on how you attacked the problem with the right solution by using all of the available information.

Q:

Careful listening and effective communication go hand in hand. Tell me about a specific time when your skill in listening helped you communicate better.

This is the interviewer's way of saying, "Okay, I liked that answer, but I'm going to ask the same question in a slightly different way—let's see what you've got. Give me another example?"

This is a clever way of ferreting out whether you were full of BS or have some substance to your answers. Give another example where you once again attend to the facts and feelings in a message, and tell how you responded in a way that related to the other person's needs in a clear, concise manner. And end with how well received your response was.

Q:

Tell me about the most complex information you ever had to read and how did you comprehend it.
Be specific.

I always like the "be specific." Translated, it means, "Don't BS me with some flowery general answer!"

We all have read stuff that gave us an instant headache (for me, it's the instruction manual that is stuffed in the box of any unassembled thing). Since the interviewer wanted "specific" (no BS), pick some technical information or research that may be applicable to the company with whom you are interviewing. Answer that you pride yourself on being able to assimilate complex technical information into a brief presentation. We all are inundated with information, so the ability to make seemingly complex information easy to understand is a very desirable trait.

Q:

This job will require you to spend a large amount of time writing. Tell me about your writing experiences that you think will contribute to your ability to do this job well.

Being an English major at Boston College, I loved this question. I would always intersperse my Technical Writing course—in which I earned an "A"—as a very helpful guide in effective written communication.

If you don't have any training in writing, answer that the most effective written communication is clear, concise, with a purpose, and, most importantly, a solution. If you have ever had anything published, bring it in your brag book and do a little show-and-tell.

Q:

You have described yourself as a problem-solver who can run the business. Give me an example.

This is a great way to demonstrate your desirable skills. Emphasize that you always use a disciplined process to define the problem, identify the root cause(s), evaluate data from a variety of sources, generate alternative solutions—and choose the best solution.

Have examples and, again, if any are in the brag book, pull 'em out. The most believable answers are the ones the interviewer can wrap his or her hands around—and see.

Q:
Tell me about your business judgment and decision-making skills.

They are looking for your ability to identify problems or opportunities and recognize symptoms, causes, and alternative solutions. Also, your ability to make timely, sound decisions even under conditions of risk and uncertainty.

You are an experienced business manager who can run the business. If you have any relevant professional training, mention it. I took a fantastic two-day seminar by Kepner-Tregoe on Problem-Solving and Decision Making, held at Harvard University. Just to mention Harvard in an interview impresses your audience (except to a Boston College guy). The course taught an effective way to determine key needs and wants and a system of ranking them in priority and then attacking the problem based on facts not on emotion.

If you don't have the time for a two-day seminar, give an example of a solution you proposed to help solve a pressing company problem.

Q:

One of the things I love about the company is that we are feedback-rich and team-based.
Describe an experience that would help you thrive in this environment.

The interviewer is looking for relationship management skills, communication, attention to detail, planning/prioritizing/goal setting, leadership, flexibility, influence, and persuasion.

Preface your answer with, "I'm glad to hear that. My current company sounds similar," and then give your example. End with, "I thrive in an environment where constructive feedback is welcomed."

Q:

Describe your leadership skills.

Demonstrate your ability to convince others to express desirable behavior and to take specific action. You pride yourself on leading by example. Integrate one or more of the following into your answer: "being able to effectively persuade, motivate, lead, empower others, negotiate, act positively, create opportunities, and influence others."

Q:
I asked you earlier about your written communication skills, but tell me about your overall communication skills.

It is clever when the interviewer pulls a Detective Columbo and sheepishly asks a question again—in a slightly different way. The interviewer is likely looking for consistency in your answer and a more general assessment of your skills in this important competency.

Answer that you pride yourself on your ability to communicate effectively in a variety of settings: one-on-one, group, and in front of a large audience. In the one-on-one and small group settings, you pride yourself on your listening skills (remember the 90 percent listening example given in one of your previous answers), your written and verbal communication skills, plus your training and experience in presenting, speaking, consulting, and updating.

Q:
Tell me how you coach and develop talent.

This is another way of asking how you manage people with a twist.

You always strive for positive reinforcement in your coaching with direct and timely feedback. You have a commitment to learning and treat each person how you would want to be treated (good old Golden Rule). Close with examples of people you have hired, trained, and promoted to greater responsibilities—and how great it made you feel.

Q:

Give me an example of your interpersonal skill level and how you applied it to overcome a difficult situation.

You want to use an example in which you illustrate your ability to "interact with others in ways that build and maintain cooperative working relationships." You "handle difficult situations using the same fundamentals as seemingly easy situations, focusing on relationship building, using a pleasant, nonthreatening demeanor and tone, with respect and tact, empathy, and above all, high integrity and ethical standards."

Q:

You will be working as a team quite often in this role, many times with a variety of functions. How do you view teamwork?

If you have examples—perhaps in your brag book, or listed on your résumé (a good idea)—use them right away. You believe in collaborative effort in order to obtain the greatest results. Be prepared to speak of some multifunctional teams you have served on, especially if you led the team.

Stress encouraging full participation of every team member where you valued differences, but, ultimately, through conflict resolution techniques, your teams always came up with creative, effective, and timely solutions to a wide range of tasks/problems.

Q:
You mentioned "initiative" earlier. Tell me about how you used initiative and creativity to solve a problem.

Try, "I pride myself on heading a problem off at the pass—before it affects business. A pro-active approach always saves the company money and increases productivity. There is always more than one alternative to solve a problem. I use creativity in my decision making and problem-solving techniques."

With my training seminar experience, when I was asked this question, I was able to answer, "My Kepner-Tregoe course taught me to list key wants and needs and then to prioritize them. This disciplined approach allowed me to creatively consider all alternatives before arriving at a decision that is fact-based and timely." If you didn't enroll in a K-T seminar, you can still use the fundamentals that I mentioned.

Q:
I like your creativity and it sounds as if you have a strong analytical side. Describe it.

Show that you summarize information well to identify and highlight key elements, patterns, results, or relationships. Have some examples of using a variety of analytical techniques to organize data. Then say you always ask a series of questions that are designed to surface additional and new information about the problem—attacking all problems from all angles—as if in 3D.

Also mention that you draw on past experience with similar situations to recognize patterns of causality. From there, you quickly separate relevant from irrelevant facts and then develop and test several hypotheses about the source of the problem.

Q:
What is your greatest accomplishment?

Does the interviewer mean personal or business? Ask the qualifier and if the answer is "both," great; if it is "pick one over the other in rank," go with business—maybe a major promotion that was a culmination of all of your hard work, accomplishments, and dedication.

Stay clear of mentioning the "birth of my first child" answer in a business interview; though it may be true—and probably should be— keep in mind that you are interviewing for a professional job.

Q:
Do you have any questions?

An important question and you always have questions. Responding, "No, I think we covered it all," gets you the boot. This is also the interviewer's not-so-subtle way of drawing the interview to a close.

This one is your last chance to leave a favorable impression. Come prepared with a notepad with at least five good questions that demonstrate your research on the company. I like the kiss-up questions here: "With the impressive results the company has had in the last five years, where do you see the company in five years?" or "I've heard some wonderful things about your company. How do you think your competitors feel about your company?" or "Customer XYZ said great things about your company and your high-quality service levels, how do other customers view you?"

After the brown-nose questions, ask, "What key skills and attributes are most needed to succeed in this job?" After the interviewer gives you the answer, plug in some examples of demonstrated success you have in each of these areas.

Testing

Many companies require mental and emotional testing of potential employees as a prerequisite to employment. Don't worry—there's not much you can do in the form of preparation—other than getting a good night's rest and having a good mindset.

I have seen companies employ a litany of tests: IQ, personality, emotional, psychological, business, math, and even testing following training (especially in pharmaceutical companies). The way I look at these tests is that if it's meant to be, it will be. Don't give yourself an ulcer over any pre-employment testing. It's not as daunting as it may seem.

Having said that, there is a strategy to employ when answering personality and emotional test questions: Be consistent.

Often you will be asked the same question three different times in three different ways. Inconsistency in your answers is usually a knock-out punch. The best advice is to consistently answer with your "business mind"—thinking about what they are looking for.

So if a company is looking for a salesperson, don't say you're timid (you'd be surprised at how many times this has happened); for a marketing manager, don't say you lack creativity; for a production position, don't say you have a difficult time with continuous tasks.

Put yourself in their shoes and answer according to the required tasks and desired traits for the position you are seeking.

Savvy Interview Techniques

One of my largest clients employed an interesting and demanding screening process. After the first interview with the hiring manager, they brought the candidate in to their headquarters for "finals." At finals, they had eight managers in different functions grill the candidate on eight different topics and then grade the performance. (I called it the "grill & grade.")

These were the eight topics (and some clarification of their meaning):

1. Cultural fit (background, interests, and work ethic)
2. Teamwork (the ability to share due credit with coworkers, display enthusiasm, and promote a friendly group environment; team spirit)
3. Planning/prioritizing/goal setting (organizational and time management skills)
4. Relationship management (interpersonal skills and the ability to work with a wide range of personality types)
5. Communication (clear thinker with strong verbal and written communication skills)

6. Leadership (the ability to assume a role of authority, advocate new insights, even when risk is involved; a role model)

7. Flexibility (the ability to adapt to a wide range of demands and an evolving work environment)

8. Influence and persuasion (the ability to clearly verbalize a position and inspire improvement)

After these eight interviews, the candidate would meet with the president and CEO who would then ask the candidate to interview him (we'll discuss this in a moment).

After this full day of interviews, the candidate would then fly to a different city to take an IQ test, personality test, and sit face-to-face with a psychiatrist who would then personally shrink test the poor slob for an hour, with questions like, "Which parent do you like the least?" Yikes! Please don't tell my mom and dad my choice, doc. He actually made one of my finalists cry with his imposing questions (she didn't get the job).

Don't fret if you are faced with a daunting selection process; be grateful that the company is so selective and have confidence in your abilities. And back to my original advice: prepare. You can imagine the difference in your "grade" if you are aware of what they are looking for ahead of time (such as their eight topics of importance) versus going in blind. Be prepared.

When the Interviewer Asks You to Interview Him or Her

This happens frequently, particularly with savvy interviewers; they can measure you by the questions you ask them. If you are prepared—and you are—this is an easy interview.

If the person is a senior manager (especially a CEO), ask strategic questions such as, *Where do you see this company in five years?* Additional questions to ask:

- *Why did you join the company?*
- *What has changed since you joined?*
- *What would you like to change?*
- *Why is the position open?*
- *What strategic advantages does your company have over your competitors?*
- *How do your customers view you?*
- *What are the first three priorities you would like to see accomplished by the person chosen to fill this position?*
- *Where does this position fit into the scheme of things?*
- *What does this company value the most and how do you think my work for you will further these values?*
- *Where do you see me in five years with this company?*
- *What's the makeup of the team in terms of experience? Will I be a mentor or will I be mentored or both?*
- *What's the most important thing I can do for this company?*
- *When top performers leave the company, why do they leave and where do they usually go?*

By now, you've answered the questions and earned an "A" grade, taken the tests and survived. Now, it's time to get the offer. It's closing time.

Closing

Usually, the interviewer will indicate that time is up.

Always ask for the job before leaving! It is a final and important opportunity to grab the job. The best "closes" are brief, direct, and spoken with confidence.

A great sample closing is this: *Do you have any concerns about my ability to do this job or any subsequent jobs with this company in the future?* If the answer is no, then reply, *When can I start?* If yes, find out what the concern is and then overcome the objection with examples of your work.

More astute interviewers may say yes just to test your mettle and see how you behave under pressure—one final time. Be confident and direct in your answer and ask for the job one last time.

What Do They Say about You after You Leave?

You've done a killer résumé, networked yourself like a Tasmanian Devil, and prepared, prepared, and prepared for the interview. Two people grilled you for over an hour. What happens when you leave?

The reality is that many interviewers hire in their own likeness. This includes hometown, religious upbringing, political affiliation, gender, ethnicity, education, and image. This doesn't mean you have to be a mirror image of the hiring manager to obtain a job offer, but the more connection you make, the greater your likelihood of nailing it.

I have heard of many behind-the-scenes discussions that make or break a person's career. The following are some avoidable derailments:

- Smelling like smoke. If the hiring manager is a nonsmoker, don't go into the interview smelling as if you just left the bowling alley on Free Cigarette Night. Many employers avoid hiring smokers due to health insurance.

- All things being equal, the more physically fit candidate usually gets hired. I heard a hiring manager say, "She was decent, but needs to lose thirty pounds." Sad but true, I knew this was the deciding factor.
- Attire. Dress conservatively and in good taste. Men should wear a suit and tie with a starched, long-sleeved dress shirt, with long dark socks and polished shoes. Women should wear a conservative suit or dress without cleavage showing, with the intention of looking professional.

Women and minorities are often at a disadvantage in the hiring process. This is not the case for a company in a diversity initiative. It is imperative that you know what you're up against. Ask your recruiter if the company is seeking women and/or minorities for the position. It may be an advantage. If not, you have to prepare that much harder. I have personally hired and placed a disproportionate number of women and minorities in jobs. This is due to the fact that women and minorities try harder, are better prepared, and have an attitude of going to get a job versus just getting interviewed.

If you notice differences between you and the hiring manager, don't panic. Try to make as many connections as you can and hope the competition is not too severe.

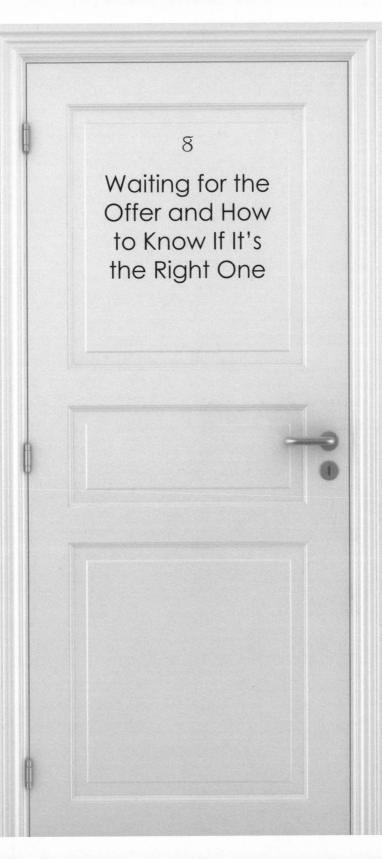

8

Waiting for the Offer and How to Know If It's the Right One

Many books I've read tell you to send a nice thank you note via the mail. If you own any of these books, put them in the recycling bin.

The thank you note is best sent via email and done as soon as possible. After the interview, the hiring manager usually makes his or her mind up within twenty-four hours. The antiquated snail mail advice (which could take five to seven days to arrive) becomes irrelevant to a potential offer. Make sure you get the business card, which contains the email address of the hiring manager, and cards from anyone else who interviewed you—each interviewer will get a separate thank you note from you.

Thank you for taking the time out of your busy schedule yesterday to discuss the opportunity at Company XYZ with me. Company XYZ's marketing provides a competitive advantage for merchants that is under-utilized. I believe that Company XYZ's Zap the Consumer product offering is well-positioned to capitalize on this opportunity in the marketplace.

My vast experience in both sales management and marketing makes me uniquely qualified for the position. I have worked with several major retailers designing and implementing successful related marketing programs. This experience would enable me to make immediate and valuable contributions to your organization.

I look forward to meeting with you in the near future to further discuss this opportunity.

Again, thank you for your time and consideration.

Sincerely,
Your name

Your thank you email should only be a few short paragraphs. Here is an actual sample thank you email that was well received—and led to an offer.

If you interviewed with more than one person, send a slightly different thank you note to each. The more you personalize it with examples from your discussion, the more sincere—and effective—it will be.

This is a critical step. Proper follow-up is expected; the thank you note is a checklist item for most interviewers. I have seen more than one candidate get clipped because he or she didn't send a thank you note. Conversely, I have seen more than one candidate win over a hiring manager who was on the fence by sending a well-written thank you note. It may make the difference in getting you an offer—or not.

Offer Time

By this stage, you probably feel as if you have run a marathon. You have placed a great deal of energy on getting to this phase: the offer. It is an exciting time and can be a little nerve-racking. Be grateful you have made it so far and that you are going to receive an offer.

If you do not receive an offer, it is a good idea to send a brief thank you note stating that you "enjoyed all your meetings with such a fine company and please consider me if an opportunity arises in the future." The person receiving the offer may say no, and an upbeat, professional note may land you the offer next.

Most offers are initially given verbally. Hiring managers either deliver them or have the executive recruiter do it. In either case, and no matter what the offer is, be grateful. Thank him or her for the offer and ask for it to be sent to you in writing (email is preferred) but mention again that you are excited about the prospect of joining such a fine company.

It's time for a little more Psych 101.

Teeter-Totter Principle

If you have worked with me as a candidate, you have undoubtedly heard of my Teeter-Totter Principle. If you haven't, bear with me. It's a very simple but apropos analogy.

Remember those days on the teeter-totter at the playground? If the other person on the teeter-totter weighed more than you, you were at a significant disadvantage. I hated to be stuck up in the air knowing I would likely crash on my bottom when the other person jumped off. Well, the job search process is like that old teeter-totter.

Before you have an interview, you are up in the air while the hiring manager is firmly on the ground. When you get an interview, you are still up in the air, but at least you're on the teeter-totter. Once you get to the final round of interviews, you are getting closer to the ground but still up in the air. Then, the offer comes. Guess where you are now? You got it: firmly on the ground. And where's the hiring manager? That's right: up in the air.

Keep this in mind: It could have taken several months to get to that offer—all the while, you were up in the air. Once the offer hits, the hiring manager expects you to say yes on the spot and start the next day. Hiring managers don't like to be up in the air for very long. They never consider the possibility that you may say no to their offer.

Even though you are on the ground, keep this teeter-totter principle in mind. If the offer feels right (follow your instincts), there is nothing wrong with verbally accepting the offer by saying, "I'm honored to have such a fine offer from you. I'm excited to work for you. Please send me the detailed offer in writing so I can formally say yes as quickly as possible."

Put the onus back on the anxious (up in the air) hiring manager, but first tell him or her that you want the job. Delaying your decision will nullify your momentum even if you eventually take the job. A verbal yes from you is not legally binding anyway—you can always change your mind if the written terms of the offer are not right.

Long live the teeter-totter!

How to Leave Your Current Company

Be 100 percent certain that you want to leave your current company before telling them. There is no turning back. So what is the best way to resign? Professionally and with dignity.

Many people do the opposite and later regret it. Saying (or singing), "Take this job and shove it!" may seem like the thing to do, but don't do it. Regardless of your unhappiness with your soon-to-be ex-boss and company, you have invested too much time and energy there to burn the bridge. Besides, if you get a poor reference years later because you had to let some anger out, was it really worth it?

Proper resignations include the following:

- Resign in person if possible. If not, you should be communicating on the phone "live"—no voicemails or emails.
- Have a letter of resignation with you (one paragraph should suffice—see sample) with your two weeks' notice spelled out and cc: Human Resources.
- Keep it professional. No personal attacks.

Sample Letter of Resignation
Dear Mr./Ms. Ex-boss,

I am resigning my position effective (today's date). I will continue to work and help in the transition process in any way I can until my final date of employment: (two weeks from today's date). I am grateful for my experiences at Company ABC and wish you and the company continued success.

Regards,
Happy X. M'Ployee
cc: Hal Phull, Human Resources

The letter of resignation is important. It is a professional way to leave on good terms—your terms. Several bosses, upon hearing you are quitting, will say, "Well, let's just make this your last day. Give me your keys and I'll have you escorted out of the building" (your boss is sure making it easy to quit with this selfish response).

By putting in your two weeks' notice, you are legally entitled to two weeks' pay, regardless of whether your boss wants you there or not. They cannot just throw you out the door without your two weeks' pay (plus unused vacation pay)—it's illegal. Resigning properly (in writing) ensures that you will get your two weeks of pay regardless of what your boss may think (this advice is worth at least what you paid for this book and then some).

Let's revisit the boss's response: He or she might lash out at you. People act selfishly and you can use this principle to your advantage. After you (professionally) told your boss, "I resign," your boss thought, "Oh no, what do I do now?" Your boss will likely want to squeeze every bit of juice out of you during your last two weeks—if he or she even keeps you there.

Take the high road: be helpful—within reason—and leverage the situation with what will help you. He or she needs you now; use this to your advantage. Ask your boss to give you a letter of recommendation on company letterhead. If you get the old I-don't-have-time excuse (complete with a four-letter word), offer to write it yourself on official company stationary and have him or her sign it. One of the best letters of recommendation I ever received was one I had to write on my own.

The letter of recommendation is important for two reasons:

1. It's a great item for your brag book (and to use in future interviews).

2. The moment you leave for the last time, bosses have a tendency of belittling you. Everything that goes wrong for the next six months will be blamed on you, and your name will usually be dragged through the mud; often, your "resignation" turns into a "we fired him or her." Egos. Having a recent letter of recommendation nullifies negative and harmful gossip.

When resigning, prepare for the worst, but expect the best. Negative thoughts, negative suggestions have no influence over you.

9

Free
Career Advice

*e*verybody likes "free stuff"—and free advice is sometimes the best. I can't be a Mystical Career Guide and Life Coach without being able to impart career (and life) advice. I'll give you some sample questions I've been asked and the advice I have given:

Q:
Can I have more than one blissful dream job?

Absolutely! You have seven items on your "narrowed down" *Bliss List* (out of your original fifteen), so you ideally could have seven dream jobs—or fifteen or twenty. There are no limits, no boundaries to what you can accomplish if you focus your mind on your goals with enthusiastic confidence and gratitude.

I have four blissful dream jobs currently—and plan on having many more. Keep in mind that it is very difficult to have more than seven things going on in your head at once—without frustrating yourself. Once you are in your bliss, you will find that other things that were on your list will magically appear. It may seem to be out of nowhere or a coincidence—at first. Remember, there are no coincidences. The Law of Attraction happens 24/7, whether you believe it (you do) or not.

Q:

Given all your experience, are there any companies you would consider "dream companies" to work for?

I think The Gallup Organization is a terrific company. *How Full Is Your Bucket?* is an easy but powerful book to read—written by Gallup's former Chairman Donald Clifton. Dr. Clifton passed away in 2003, but his legacy—of an outstanding culture—has continued. Dr. Clifton wrote the book on positive psychology literally, starting in the 1950s. Then he put it into practice at Gallup. If you want a very positive environment (filled with genuine appreciation and gratitude), a low turnover rate, and high employee loyalty and morale, then Gallup is atop the list.

Other fine dream companies to target? Every year, Fortune lists the 100 Best Companies to Work For. The top ten from 2009 are these:

1. NetApp
2. Edward Jones
3. Boston Consulting
4. Google
5. Wegmans Food Market

6. Cisco Systems

7. Genentech

8. Methodist Hospital System

9. Goldman Sachs

10. Nugget Market

Q:

My daughter is graduating from college soon, can you help her?

Sure! Though I work primarily with senior-level management job searches (usually with total compensation over $100,000), I'd love to help your daughter. What would she like to do?

"She's not sure, but her degree is in business," you say.

Great. The world is her oyster. I'm guessing she has not given much serious thought to what she wants to do with her B.S. (I always think the BS is aptly named and funny. For the record, I have a B.A. degree. I didn't get my BS until I went into sales.)

My advice is to have her try to find a large company. Which ones? Have her start with the Fortune top 10 companies:

1. Wal-Mart Stores

2. Exxon Mobil

3. Chevron

4. General Motors

5. ConocoPhillips

6. General Electric

7. Ford Motor

8. Citigroup
9. Bank of America
10. AT&T

The largest companies offer the greatest opportunities for career growth and are likely to be doing business for the next ten years. Also, they will have extensive college recruitment efforts and salaries that are competitive if not above average.

Your daughter should target these companies with creative networking (I know it may not be easy), direct mail, and via each company's website. Most importantly, find out which of these companies will conduct on-campus interviews and get on the schedule. Many colleges and universities offer a Career Night—when sometimes hundreds of companies send representatives (usually human resources and/or sales managers) to recruit students. These are a must to attend!

Have your daughter dress in a conservative suit, bring a folder full of résumés, and be first in line. Have her treat these brief meetings as an interview. She should express genuine interest in the company and be brief but effective: "I'm so glad you came here tonight—and that I had a chance to meet you. I am interested in interviewing for a position with your company. What are the next steps?"

This type of interaction opens the door and gives your daughter a card with a phone number and email address for follow-up, plus a face-to-face meeting. Chances are, the person at Career Night will be doing the on-campus interviewing, and your daughter now has left a favorable first impression.

If location doesn't matter, my advice, especially to a college graduate, but also applicable to anyone, is move to Bentonville, Arkansas, and get a job with Wal-Mart (there are plenty of positions available in all departments). The training programs that Wal-Mart offers are solid; opportunity for advancement is strong; but salaries for companies looking for people to work with Wal-Mart and live in Bentonville,

Arkansas, are way out of whack. You can expect to earn, on average, 30 percent more in salary working for a company (and there are plenty of them) doing business—or wanting to do business—with good ole Wal-Mart. Plus, the cost of living is very low and quality of life is very high.

A couple of years spent in Bentonville will catapult you up corporate ladders with companies. You cannot become a vice president of a consumer goods' manufacturer without Wal-Mart knowledge and experience. They are number one and will stay number one. They already account for more than 20 percent (sometimes 30 to 40 percent) of most of their vendors'/companies' total revenue.

Other locations to consider where salaries are high relative to the cost of living and the quality of life are

- Redmond, Washington (Microsoft #44)
- Minneapolis, Minnesota (Target #31)
- Cincinnati, Ohio (P&G #23)

Q:
I am a female [or minority] seeking a career change. Can you help me?

Absolutely! Many companies hire recruiters especially for diversity initiatives. Ask your recruiter if he or she is working on any searches for minority candidates. It is usually an advantage to have minority status. This was not the case thirty years ago. Nowadays, however, a qualified minority candidate can sometimes earn a higher salary by lining up multiple offers. The best litmus test is to ask what percentage of employees are minority status in a given company and how many senior managers are minorities. A company with a low percentage of minorities may be a red flag (you'd feel like a unicorn) or a golden opportunity for rapid advancement.

Q:

My ideal job is to be the CEO of a Fortune 500 company. What is the ideal background needed?

Great question. Big company training is paramount to learning the fundamentals and giving you the impressive, blue-chip background. From there, multi-company and multi-industry exposure is critical.

If you can "survive" with one company for your entire career, you are a very rare breed—but not likely a candidate for CEO—with perceived myopic, one-dimensional experience.

The chairman of a Fortune 10 company was asked by an employee, "What would it take for me to become chairman here?"

The chairman retorted, "Leave the company."

He wasn't joking either. Seek multi-company exposure, and when you change companies, commit to yourself that you will do so only if you can ascend to greater responsibility. CEOs become CEOs by making strategic, career-building moves—emulate their actions.

Q:

When is the best time to look for a new job?

While you're gainfully employed. You have the most leverage when you don't have to leave. Companies are looking for successful, well-adjusted, and optimistic people. You are more likely to gain the next step in responsibility and a higher income if you can show an attitude of "I care, but not that much."

Q:
How do I know when I am making the right move?

I was asked this question by a friend whose company was just placed on the chopping block (we call it putting up the corporate *For Sale* sign). He was panicky and full of fear for the future (hint, it's not Eckhart Tolle).

He had gotten an offer to work two levels below where he currently was and for a company with a less-than-stellar reputation. He was ready to jump ship and asked for my blessing. My initial reaction was to call him "nuts," but my advice was "make your job change only if the job you are accepting would make sense for your career goals, regardless of whether your company is for sale or not."

His fear reflected his insecurity, and he was irrational (not a good reference point). He ended up ignoring my advice and grabbing that job. And he was miserable right away. He only lasted four months—then he was fired.

So, now, where is he? Interviewing from the unenviable position of two levels below his actual market value—and unemployed. Applying the Law of Attraction to his case: he got what he wished for.

If a job makes sense whether or not you are unemployed or are about to become unemployed, take the job. Otherwise, set your career goals and keep looking with enthusiastic confidence.

Q:

What makes you a successful executive recruiter?

Two things: I seek quality companies to represent and quality candidates to place.

I only recruit for companies that I would work for myself. Interestingly, I frequently get job offers for the very position from companies looking to use me as their recruiter—I tell them they "can't afford me." I look at companies from all angles.

Sir Warren Buffett is a great inspiration for me. His investment decisions are based on common sense—he needs to really understand and like the products or services of the companies he invests in and they have to have superior management. Finally, he has to be able to predict with certainty where the business will be ten years from now. He is also a voracious reader. He's read more annual reports than anyone. Once he "gets it," he moves quickly. He is rarely wrong.

My target companies (like Buffett's) need to have a competitive advantage (number one or two in their industries), stability, and growth that I believe will happen. I also look for a positive corporate culture with low turnover—the numbers rarely lie. I have worked for (as an employee) and recruited for a large number of privately-held companies. They tend to view business in the long term, are very passionate about what they do, have great stability, and have lower-than-average turnover.

Once I'm contracted to work on their behalf as their executive recruiter, I view myself as an employee of the company. I always have enthusiasm for my clients and view them as friends and not clients.

When it comes to candidates, I pride myself on having the highest quality database in the industry. I have built up an impressive list of people by using referrals. When I speak to a candidate I respect, I always ask him or her to recommend other topnotch people, regardless of location and function. "Like attracts like" and good people know other good people who know other good people and on and on.

When I'm given a search assignment, I have the capability to pinpoint "A"-rated people with a few clicks on my mouse. Using my custom-designed electronic referral notes, I am then targeting people who have been pre-referenced—usually without their knowledge. I always laugh when a hiring company, at offer time, wants to make a "reference check" as a condition for employment. References provided by the candidate aren't going to reveal any aha's. Hello—they're provided by the candidate (and if the candidate has a pulse, his or her references are told what to say, making this step useless).

A smart company should require a recruiter to *pre*-reference all potential employees. Earlier, I mentioned the importance of helping a recruiter (only if you trust them) by providing names of good people if you're not interested in the job personally. This is gold for me. You are automatically elevated in my database if you help me. Boomerang?

Quality companies and quality candidates allow me to deliver quality work.

Q:
Will talking to executive recruiters hurt my career?

It shouldn't. A professional executive recruiter would always maintain confidentiality. After reading the earlier section, however, you know that many are not trustworthy. Be careful with information you give out to a recruiter. If he or she doesn't earn your trust, don't trust your personal information with him or her.

As a general rule, do not send your résumé to a recruiter unless he or she identifies the position and company to you and it is something you are interested in pursuing. There are plenty of horror stories about recruiters trying to use a current employee's résumé as leverage to recruit for the very company that pays the paycheck. Be wary of the recruiter who requests your résumé without any specifics.

Q:

Is it safe to send my résumé to an Internet service?

No! Never post your résumé, name, or your identity that may give you away on any Internet service. Human resource departments (and bosses) have been known to scour online services looking for their employees' résumés. Chances are, if a boss spends his time looking for his employees' résumés online rather than working with them, you don't want to work for him anyway. But don't give him a reason to let you go.

Q:

I recently graduated from college and am thinking of getting my master's degree. I have a couple of interesting job offers currently. What should I do?

Isn't it great to have options? There is something to be said for completing all of your education and then obtaining that dream job with advanced degree in hand. In most jobs, the greater the degree, the greater the responsibility—and pay. But given the ridiculous cost of education (especially for a top-tier MBA from a private school), it is a great idea to gain valuable work experience (and a paycheck for a change) and have the company pay for it.

Many companies (especially the larger ones) have fantastic education reimbursement programs. And many graduate programs offer flexible accelerated degrees (with weekend/night combinations).

If you don't mind multi-tasking for eighteen months (or fewer in many cases), you can get a free MBA and have a built-in career launch pad once you graduate. Companies will promote you faster when you obtain an advanced degree; they know you are more marketable and could flee to one of their competitors if they don't put you on their fast track.

I took a graduate course toward an MBA degree while working full-time during my first year out of college. I was in the middle of an intensive management training schedule with my company and was actually able to double-dip. I tied in the primary required project for the course (a written case study and presentation to the class) with my management training. I earned an "A" grade and impressed some top brass at the company with my independent research. And it only took a handful of nights during one summer. The company paid for the course, I was promoted a few months later, the course helped, and it was well worth it.

Take the best job offer from the company that has the best education-reimbursement policy and negotiate a graduate degree–reimbursement benefit before you accept the offer (many companies try to make you go through an "approval process" before shelling out money for your courses, especially if it's an expensive executive MBA program).

Q:
Why did you go into business for yourself?

As I transitioned from college/graduate school into the business world, one of my early *Top Seven Bliss List* items was to be self-employed. Every company I worked for was rock solid as I joined, but every single one either sold outright or divested the division I was in. This strengthened my desire to own my own company one day. I figured, I may as well start my own company; at least I'll know if it's going to sell.

Q:
What if I'm asked if I'm still employed during the interview and I'm not?

The right answer is to be truthful, but be prepared to give a very good explanation as to why.

An effective answer is: "As you probably know, my company is in the midst of a sizable layoff. I'm likely to receive an offer for early retirement, even though I'm obviously too young to retire. I am interested in your company and the position regardless of my company's layoff decisions/ offers. Ideally, I could time a severance package accordingly."

You were vague enough without directly lying (it's none of their business and has no bearing on the work you would do for them anyway). Plus, there isn't an interviewer around who wouldn't be impressed with your ability to first collect a severance package and then come to his or her company. This answer makes your stock rise in the interviewer's eyes.

Q:

I'm close to getting an offer from another company. Should I leverage a better deal from my current company?

Whoa! Putting a gun to your boss's head with, "If you don't match this, I'm outta here," is never a good idea. You just read the teeter-totter principle; it applies here also.

It is wiser to approach your boss—as you are interviewing for a job elsewhere—with, "I am having career indecision and I wanted to discuss my future, projected responsibilities, including compensation, with you." Never, ever say you have an offer from another company and demand that your current company match it or else you're outta here— and expect your boss to help you now or long term. This is a form of a counteroffer request and *counteroffers don't work.*

What is a counteroffer? It's when you tell your current company that you are resigning and they talk you out of leaving, usually by tossing you more money to stay. If you decide to do an about face and stay, the odds are against you.

The Wall Street Journal had a great article about the pitfalls of counteroffers. They studied twenty-nine people in differing jobs and industries who took counteroffers in a given year. Twenty-seven out of the twenty-nine were either fired, let go, downsized, or right-sized within the first year. The other two were unhappy and were looking furiously for another job. There's a teeter-totteresque explanation for this. Here we go again.

When you tell your boss the two magic words, "I resign," you hope he or she will be the consummate professional and say something like, "We're really going to miss you here, but I am excited for you. Good luck and tell me if there's anything I can do." Nope! Most bosses' first reaction is, "Oh, no, what am I gonna do now? You can't leave me high and dry."

Remember, people usually operate from their id-ego, a selfish state, and automatically take a resignation as a personal affront. They know they will get a hard time from their bosses for losing you. If they've experienced turnover in the past, they also know it will take them six months (on average) to replace you. And, at this point, they will do whatever they can to coax you to stay.

When I resigned from one of the companies I had worked for, they tried to coax me to stay with more money. Ironically, this was the same company that had underpaid me for five of the last seven years, was in a 40 percent downsizing, and had frozen all salary increases. Now, all of a sudden after I found an ideal job with more money and greater responsibility, they could find some dough to throw from those "budgets" that didn't exist earlier.

I said, "Thanks, but no thanks." Had I taken a counteroffer, I know they would have let me go during the downsizing (one of my mentors told me this a couple of years later). I followed my instincts—and they were right.

Counteroffers are nothing more than a short-term fix for your boss to find your replacement! The percentages are stacked against you. If you have taken a counteroffer, turn up your job search before you become another statistical victim.

See Your Retirement Party

This exercise is a powerful way to attract your desired dream job. This one involves visualization (best done during meditation or quiet thought).

See yourself seated at the head table for your retirement party. You are electing to retire on your own, and your dream company is honoring you! See each person get up and describe how you touched their lives, accomplished amazing things, and were an inspiration to so many people. Be creative—use your *Bliss List*.

The more realistic you can make your retirement party, the better. Even though you're much older in your visualization, see yourself at your retirement party as vibrant, energetic, and grateful. The more intensely you can feel as if it is really happening, the stronger your vibration, which will ultimately trigger the Universe to answer.

Q:
I'm fifty-eight years old and looking for a career change. Am I too old?

Don't ever ask a recruiter or potential employer this question. It is illegal for an employer to ask a potential employee his or her age. However, as an executive recruiter, I am asked that question by clients (hiring companies) often, regarding candidates. Legally, I cannot ask age either. It's ironic: it's illegal to ask the question, but you can require the same person to fill out an application for employment and happen to include date of birth. The cold, hard reality of the business world is that youth is desirable.

Generally, hiring managers prefer to hire in their own likeness—looking for similar/same company background/training, hometown, religion, race and/or age group. Like attracts like—remember. In this case, find out the age of the hiring manager (that's not illegal) and his or her boss, and if you think age is an issue, then "modify" (not lie!) your résumé. The hiring manager only needs to look at college degree and date to get an idea of your age. So don't include the year you graduated. Remember, it's your résumé and your marketing document.

The next giveaway is the first year you worked after graduation. Since you have to give at least some years for employment, omit your first ten years after college; chances are, they are irrelevant anyway. You are not lying, just appearing ten years younger—on paper. For the interview, be careful not to divulge dates that would give the nosy interviewer the answer to the "illegal" question. If you are designed to live to one-hundred twenty, being fifty-eight should be the prime of your life, after all.

The irony is that the older employee is generally wiser and, in many cases, more productive and loyal. Napoleon Hill, author of one of the bestselling business books of all time, *Think and Grow Rich,* believed a person made the most intelligent decisions in his or her mid-fifties.

But most companies want young and implicitly perceived, energetic new hires. The desired formula is to hire someone for five years, work them hard, and then boot them out the door—and then replace them with a young hot-shot. At all the companies I worked for, there weren't many retirement parties. The days of getting the gold watch at age sixty-five and walking out proudly on your own are over.

Employers are not loyal to employees and vice versa (gives a guy like me in executive search a chance to make a buck or two—or $3 million). This is true in most industries and professions, and is likely to continue or even worsen.

The Questions about Illegal Questions

Though it is very useful to learn as much as you can about the hiring manager and his or her boss, never divulge personal information about yourself unless it is to your advantage. It is illegal for an employer to discriminate against you based on your race, gender, religion, marital status, age, disabilities, ethnic background, country of origin, sexual preferences, or age.

Does it still happen? Sure. But you are not required to answer illegal questions. If asked one, simply say, in a lighthearted way, "I'm not sure we should be discussing this. Can we stick to my skills to do the job you are interviewing me for?"

Any hiring manager who asks these questions is unprofessional, unenlightened, and has poor business etiquette. My advice: turn and run. Do you really want to work there?

Q:

I was unemployed for nine months. What should I do about the gap?

Many people list dates in months and years and this poses a problem. If you took time off from the workplace to raise children, this raises a red flag.

On your résumé, list dates in years only (without months) so any gaps shouldn't even be noticed. If you took five years off to raise children, consider leaving dates off entirely. You can deemphasize your dates—*italicize* and don't bold them. Place them in parentheses next to the job title rather than stand alone (and stand out). If you did some work (hopefully this is the case), erase the gap with placing yourself as a "Management Consultant."

We've covered a wide gamut of information. I hope you have been formulating and fine-tuning your own career goals. There are plenty of sources for advice—both paid and free. The ultimate barometer for accepting advice is your instinct. If it is right for you, you will feel it. Trust your gut instincts—they are always right.

10

Marching Orders

Dream your job
   Make it real

First with goals
   Then with feel

Close your eyes
   And see the sky

As you fly
   Don't ask why

The life you choose
   Unreal may seem

Build your life
   With your dream

W hile studying English (and many of the great masters of the language), I told more than one professor that one day I would write and publish a poem. It may not be Shakespeare, but it's mine, and I did it! Touché, Billy-boy.

I have really enjoyed taking you through *The Bliss List*. I hope you are inspired to live the life you were meant to live—with abundance and joy. Combining the mystical (the inner wisdom you have) with the practical (actionable insight) will catapult you into any world you choose to create for yourself.

Buddha said, "An idea that is developed and put into action is more important than an idea that exists only as an idea." Notice ideas that come to you and follow your emotions. If the idea feels good inside, put it into action. You have all the tools to join the one out of five of us who are "happy" in our jobs.

You know that you control it—you have the power to become a disciplined mind, devoid of limitation and toxic thought. You are energetic, abundant, and joyful; the more you unleash your inner core, the better your job—and your life—becomes.

We're nearing the end of the book. One of my initial *Bliss List* items was to help more than 100,000 people; thank you for bringing me one step closer to my goal. Life's about the journey, not the destination. Thank you for being part of my journey and for sharing yours with me. Everyone is connected. We are all brothers and sisters; mothers and fathers; or sons and daughters.

I am eternally grateful that you made the time to finish *The Bliss List*. I sincerely hope you are inspired by this book and will try the many things you have read for yourselves. They work. When they work for you—when you obtain your bliss—please tell me your story and what helped you on your journey (I smell a sequel). Send to: JPHansen@ YourBlissList.com and visit www.YourBlissList.com for updates.

Mother Teresa said, "God doesn't require us to succeed; He only requires that you try." You have the tools and inspiration; now it's time to try.

Good luck in finding your bliss. Sharing this with you has actually become my newest blissful dream job. Thank you for sharing my dream.

One final note: change is eternal, progress divine. Be your bliss!

Résumé
Makeovers

M eet Barb. Barb was let go (out of the blue and with no warning) from a huge Fortune 100 pharmaceutical company. She hadn't kept up her résumé (understatement) and was in a bit of a panic when she called me, since she was feeling pressure to obtain employment—and fast.

She's a well-paid sales executive, earning almost $200,000 in the most current year. Here is the original résumé she sent me. Does her résumé reflect that she is worth that much? I don't think so.

After speaking with Barb for about a half hour, I realized her résumé didn't reflect how well she was verbalizing her accomplishments either. This résumé, by her own admission, was "thrown together quickly." I asked, "Do you want *thrown together quickly* to keep you unemployed *indefinitely*?" Barb didn't laugh. I told her that it wouldn't take her very long to transform her résumé into something she was proud to use.

Her dilemma (and it wasn't a bad one to have): she had an interview lined up in three days for a great job—a different and more lucrative area of her industry with a well-respected company. She knew she had to work on her résumé—a lot. I gave her my tested résumé advice: "Use sentences in paragraph form to clearly describe the activities and bullet points to highlight what you accomplished." (Sound familiar? If not, you better turn back to chapter 3 and reread.)

Here's Barb's original, thrown-together résumé. The makeover follows.

BEFORE

BARB E. DAHL
31 South Main Street
Anytown, NJ 10012
609-200-0000 cellular
609-211-1111 home
bdahl@salesqueen.net

EMPLOYMENT:

6/04–8/08   **Pfeel Well Pay More, Inc.,**–Anytown,
NJ Senior Therapeutic Specialty Representative
Manage territory consisting of Anytown1/Anytown2: Methodist Hospital, All Well Health System, Anytown: St Elizabeth's Hospital, Bryant East and West, Freeme, Kowtown, and Havenot, New Jersey.
Call on specialty physicians i.e. general surgeons, orthopedic surgeons, neurologists, pain medicine, pulmonary/critical care, hospitalists, and emergency room physicians to increase product use and market share; develop and implement business plan, call cycle, and speaker activities within territory to insure coverage with respect to strategic capabilities; assist DM with training and mentoring two new representatives; support DM with setting up preceptorships and presenting POA topics.

7/02–6/04   **Slimmer Orthopedics**–Anytown, NJ
Territory Manager
Responsible for selling full line of orthopedic implants and trauma products to 9 hospitals and 2 surgery centers. In charge of negotiating prices for instruments, implants, and competitive conversions. Oversee use of Slimmer Orthopedics re-infusion products with spine and joint surgeons in Anytown. Present in surgery to support surgeons and staff in correct use of Slimmer Orthopedics instruments and implants. Conduct training session for surgical technicians and surgery staff on proper use of Slimmer equipment.

10/96–7/02   **Pfeel Well Pay More, Inc.,**–Anytown, NJ
Senior Institutional Healthcare Representative
Successfully sold all products in a variety of settings including:
Academic Medicine; University of New Jersey Medical Center, Clarkstein Hospital, Princeton University Medical Center
Federal Accounts; Anytown VAMC, Skyblue Air Force Base
Long Term Care; Ominouscare, Unicare, Kohlsteins
Managed Care; United Healthcare, Coventry, Blue Cross/Blue Shield
2001 IHR LAT MVP

BEFORE

Tryit Convention winner 1998
Zittec Convention winner 1998
Arthriticept Convention winner 1997
- 1998 VPC (#1 IHR in Region)
- 1998 Circle of Excellence (#6 in Division)
- 1998 IHR Rookie of the Year
- 1998 IHR Mover and Shaker Award winner (greatest change in GAR position)

7/89–10/96 **Wellfunded Financial**–Anytown, NJ
Compliance Auditor (10/95–10/96)
Oversee compliance functions of 28 consumer finance offices in eight Eastern States;
perform compliance audits and cash integrity reviews and report findings to District

Managers and Executive Officers.

Branch Manager (7/89–10/95)
Manage and maintain $9 million finance office. Train and supervise staff of 7 in all
aspects of daily business; approve and underwrite all lending and insurance decisions; set
and oversee goals in order to meet employee and branch objectives; coordinate marketing
plans for customers to accomplish branch goals; review all reports concerning trends and
dealer activity to access areas of need or concern.

ORGANIZATIONS: International Credit Association
United Way Volunteer
Big Brothers/Big Sisters Volunteer

EDUCATION: **Perfect State College**–Perfect, NJ
Bachelor of Science, May 1989
Major: Business Administration/Marketing
Overall GPA: 3.55/4.0 **Major GPA:**3.76/4.0
- Memorial Basketball Scholarship
- Perfect State College Basketball Scholarship -3 yr letter award
- Perfect State College Baseball Scholarship -3 yr letter award
- Rotary Club-Susie Dingbat Scholarship
- Academic Honors List
- Varsity Club President
- Phi Beta Landing Business Sorority

Did you notice she used sentence descriptions and bullet points for
one of her jobs but not the other three? It was the first thing I noticed.
And you can bet it would be the first thing the hiring manager would
notice—just before she crumples it up and tosses it in the round file.
You cannot use an inconsistent format on your résumé, whether you
follow my advice or not; it's one or the other.

The good news was that the toughest part of the résumé improvement
process was over. She mentioned several outstanding accomplishments
while we were talking, yet none of them were on her résumé. I told her

all she had to do was to write what she had just told me. Later the same day, Barb sent over this improved version:

AFTER

BARB E. DAHL
31 South Main Street
Anytown, NJ 10012
609-200-0000 cellular
bdahl@salesqueen.net

EMPLOYMENT:

Pfeel Good Pay More, Inc., –Anytown, NJ   6/04–Present

Senior Therapeutic Specialty Representative–Anytown, NJ

Manage territory consisting of Anytown1/Anytown2: Methodist Hospital, All Well Health System, Anytown: St Elizabeth's Hospital, Bryant East and West, Freeme, Kowtown, and Havenot, New Jersey. Call on Specialty Physicians: General Surgeons, Orthopedic Surgeons, Neurologists, Pain Medicine, Pulmonary/Critical Care, Hospitalists, Endocrinologists, and Emergency Room Physicians to increase product use and market share; develop and implement business plan, call cycle, and speaker activities within territory to insure coverage with respect to strategic capabilities.

- Ranked #1 (out of 10) in District sales of Zittec–$2.3 million.
- Increased sales by 64% for Zittec over last year in #1 Zip Code, 10010–Anytown, NJ.
- Increased sales by 151% for Zittec over last year in #2 Zip Code, 10011, Beggan Mercy Medical Center.
- Increased Market Share of Zittec by 62.5%.
- Increased Market Share of Vfriend by 12.6% over last year.
- Currently at 110% of Zittec quota (#1 weighted product).
- Successfully launched 9 different drugs across 4 different medical specialties.

Slimmer Orthopedics–Warsaw, IN   7/02–6/04

Territory Manager—Anytown, NJ

Responsible for selling full line of orthopedic implants and trauma products to 9 hospitals and 2 surgery centers. In charge of negotiating prices for instruments, implants, and competitive conversions. Oversee use of Slimmer re-infusion products with spine and joint surgeons in Anytown. Present in surgery to support surgeons and staff in correct use of Slimmer instruments and implants. Conduct training session for surgical technicians and surgery staff on proper use of Slimmer equipment.

- Ranked #1 in class of 30 for Slimmer hip and knee training in Warsaw, IN.
- Successfully converted Faith Regional Hospital, Norfolk, NE to Slimmer trauma products. Successfully converted #1 Orthopedic Surgeon in Bohmfalk, NJ to Slimmer hip products—took volume from zero to $375,000 in first full year as Territory Manager.
- Increased territory volume from $560,000 to $980,000 in first full year as Territory Manager.

Pfeel Good Pay More, Inc., –Anytown, NJ   10/96–7/02

Senior Institutional Healthcare Representative–Anytown, NJ

Successfully sold all products in a variety of settings including: **Academic Medicine:** University of New Jersey Medical Center, Clarkstein Hospital, Princeton University Medical Center **Federal Accounts:** Anytown VAMC, Skyblue Air Force Base **Long Term Care:** Ominouscare, Unicare, Kohlsteins **Managed Care:** United Healthcare, Coventry, Blue Cross/Blue Shield.

AFTER

BARB E. DAHL

- 2001 IHR LAT **MVP.**
- Tryit Convention winner 1998.
- Zittec Convention winner 1998.
- Arthriticept Convention winner 1997.
- 1998 VPC (#1 IHR in Region).
- 1998 Circle of Excellence.
- 1998 IHR **Rookie of the Year.**
- 1998 IHR Mover and Shaker Award winner (greatest change in GAR position).

Wellfunded Financial–Anytown, NJ   07/89–10/96

Compliance Auditor   10/95–10/96

Oversee compliance functions of 28 consumer finance offices in eight Eastern States; perform compliance audits and cash integrity reviews and report findings to District Managers and Executive Officers.

Branch Manager   07/89–10/95

Manage and maintain $9 million finance office. Train and supervise staff of seven in all aspects of daily business; approve and underwrite all lending and insurance decisions; set and oversee goals in order to meet employee and branch objectives; coordinate marketing plans for customers to accomplish branch goals; review all reports concerning trends and dealer activity to access areas of need or concern.

ORGANIZATIONS:

United Way Volunteer, 2005–2006
Big Brothers/Big Sisters Volunteer, 2001–2003

ADDITIONAL TRAINING:

Pharmacology One
Pfeel Good Pay More Sales
Pfeel Good Pay More Institutional Selling IV
Pfeel Good Pay More Specialty Selling V
Targeted Selection
Associate Sales Director I
Evelyn Wood Speed Reading
"Converting to Yes" Pfeel Good Pay More Advanced Sales

EDUCATION:

Perfect State College–Perfect, NJ
Bachelor of Science, May 1989
Major: Business Administration/Marketing
Overall GPA: 3.55/4.0 **Major GPA:** 3.76/4.0
- Memorial Basketball Scholarship
- Perfect State College Basketball Scholarship -3 yr letter award
- Perfect State College Baseball Scholarship -3 yr letter award
- Rotary Club-Susie Dingbat Scholarship
- Academic Honors List
- Varsity Club President
- Phi Beta Landing Business Sorority

PERSONAL: Married, 1 child

Notice a difference? Barb had articulated all of her accomplishments well, and now she listed them on her most important step in the process—the résumé. She created more space and gave the résumé a full appearance by dropping the titles below the respective companies. She made the date of her last job "Present," which got her over that hurdle of explaining why she wasn't with the company anymore (she was still collecting a paycheck in the form of severance pay and unused vacation pay so, technically, she was still there).

She blocked the right side of her résumé to match the left by changing from "left justify" to "full justify" (from the Microsoft Word toolbar). She added "Additional Training" which shows the interviewer that Barb is well-trained.

I wasn't a fan of Barb's original "Organizations" section. It's never advantageous to tell a future employer that you are loaded up with outside, time-consuming, and unrelated interests. Barb wanted to show her philanthropic side, so we compromised by scaling it back to two organizations, and we put it in the past tense by placing end dates on each one. This tells the employer, "Hey, I'm a good person by volunteering to two very important causes, but I'm free and clear now to put all my energies toward working for you."

These résumé changes were not too severe, but it was the difference between getting a blissful dream job paying over $200,000 versus not even getting an interview. It took Barb less than one hour to make these changes. The result: she nailed it and won the job offer! I would say this was a good return on investment.

Don't ever underestimate the power of your true first impression—your résumé!

Meet Pat Peoples. This résumé would not get to the top of the pile, and it may find the round file. Like Barb's original, Pat's was lacking accomplishments. It was overkill on bullet points, but they were not used to accentuate accomplishments. Using bullet points for everything dilutes their impact.

I'm also not a big fan of the "Objective" as I discussed earlier. They're usually too general (like Pat's) and don't really add anything. If an item on a résumé doesn't add anything, it detracts from your first impression. The proper "Objective" would be listing your ideal job by title, but it is not a needed item. My advice: "Get rid of it and use the extra space for impactful accomplishments."

I also don't like the "Summary." It says, "I know you won't really read my résumé so I'll give you the same information twice." Lose the "Summary" and stick with the recommended format: list activities in sentence form, and then bullet-point your accomplishments in order of importance.

In addition, Pat's résumé was convoluted, bouncing around with accomplishments and responsibilities with no cohesiveness. It also employed passive words like *executed, implemented, conducted,* and *serviced.* If you are trying to paint yourself as a hard-charger and a winner, then passive words won't cut it. Not many employers say, "Get me someone who is a good implementer! A real executer. Someone who can conduct things and service an existing client."

My advice: use action words such as *successfully sold, created, developed, obtained, ranked #1, earned,* and *launched.*

Judge for yourself. Then we'll look at the makeover.

BEFORE

Pat Peoples
1700 N. Capital Blvd. ■ (Anyplace, TX 78746 ■ ((310) 706-0123) ■ patpeoples@always.com

OBJECTIVE

A challenging career in outside sales where I can utilize my extensive experience and skills in sales, marketing, communication, and networking to achieve the highest company, career, and personal goals.

SUMMARY
- Over ten years of successful sales experience with six years in solution selling (multimedia, print, e-commerce advertising, and search engine optimization and marketing services)
- Proven ability to increase sales and maximize profitability by:
  - Creating and implementing innovative sales strategies and customized product/service offerings and proposals
  - Consistently building a solid pipeline of qualified prospects by cold calling, cultivating leads and developing referrals
  - Establishing strong, long-term client and agency relationships through excellent customer service
  - Maintaining extensive product and market knowledge
- Adept at cold calling, prospecting, negotiating & closing business, and account management/ development
- Ability to manage existing operations through changes in technology, product repositioning, and various financial environments
- Effective leader, self-starter, problem-solver, and team player dedicated to exceeding goals
- Proficient in Microsoft Office (Word, Excel, PowerPoint, Outlook,) sales management software, and numerous software, hardware, and internet products/services
- Knowledge of online advertising technologies, including third party ad serving, rich media, and emerging ad-targeting and search technology

PROFESSIONAL EXPERIENCE

Perfectmix, Chicago, IL 2006 to present
(Performance-Based Marketing Division of Demonink)
Account Executive South West Region
- Develop and close deals with top brand marketers to sell their products/services via Perfectmix Paid Search Marketing, Search Engine Optimization, and Affiliate Marketing Services
- Work collaboratively and effectively with all levels of staff including senior management, marketing, and external strategic business partner contacts at Google and Yahoo! & top advertising agencies
- Construct customized presentations and proposals using competitive intelligence and marketing data from third party resources such as HitWise, AdGooRoo, Forrester, Yahoo! Buzz, & Comscore
- Present proprietary search technology and competitive advantages to Vice Presidents of Marketing of top retailers and companies such as CBS, Epson, Disney, Mazda, Countrywide, Guess, Toyota, etc.
- Accomplishments:
  - Achieved quarterly business objectives and sales goals

Los Angeles Grind, Los Angeles, CA 1999 to 2006
Senior Account Executive
- Aggressively developed Southern California market for internet recruiting services, banner advertisements, and multi media campaigns for Fortune 500 and 1000 companies

BEFORE

- Launched Careerbuilder.com in So. California market in 1999; successfully grew Los Angeles Grind market share to become the #1 Tribune newspaper for Careerbuilder sales for five consecutive years
- Educated VP's, decision makers and agencies to emerging online technology and innovation while supporting the benefits and need for multimedia recruitment and branding strategies
- Repositioned competitive role against industry leaders such as Monster.com and HotJobs.com
- Trained, mentored, and motivated Recruitment Classifieds Division to drive sales by developing sales skills and online advertising product knowledge
- Most sales involve annual or semi-annual commitment. Client list includes Boeing, Mitsubishi, Healthnet, Northrop Grumman, Corinthian Colleges, Ameriquest
- Accomplishments and Awards:
    - Achieved #1 Online Sales Person Classifieds Division 2004; 132% Quota 2005
    - Exceeded yearly quota for 5 consecutive years by 128% to 165%
    - Awarded Los Angeles Times 2001 Online Sales Person of the Year
    - Earned #1 Sales Person CalendarLive 1999, 2000

GoodFood.com, San Francisco, CA   **1997 to 1999**
Regional Sales Representative
- Established new Southern California territory and collaborated in designing the sales strategy and training collateral that grew company sales force from 4 to 60 representatives nationwide
- Executed sales through effective cold calling, canvassing, lead generation, and referral programs
- Created and implemented regional sales and marketing strategies to consistently grow new customer base to 180 new customers first year
- Clients consisted of numerous restaurant chains including Dominos, Brinker International, Patina
- Accomplishments and Awards:
    - Produced top sales in the region and 4th in the nation (out of 60 sales representatives) in 1998 generating 9.2% of the company's annual revenue

Equiscam International, Inc., Las Vegas, NV   **1995 to 1997**
Sales and Marketing Representative
- Conducted sales presentations, product trainings, and negotiated contracts with clients
- Serviced existing accounts which included restaurants, real estate developers, and other commercial businesses
- Established and expanded client database through cold calling and client referral programs
- Accomplishments:
    - Achieved the ranking of the top 3 sales representative in the nation June 1996

EDUCATION

BS Psychology / Cum Laude Texas A&M University 1993
2001-2005 Careerbuilder.com Bi-annual Training Seminars
2000 Non-Manipulative Selling
1999 SPIN Selling
1993-1994 University of North Texas
        Masters Graduate Program

AFTER

Pat Peoples
1700 N. Capital Blvd. ■ (Anyplace, TX 78746 ■ ((310) 706-0123) ■ patpeoples@always.com

PROFESSIONAL EXPERIENCE

Perfectmix, Chicago, IL   2006 to present
(Performance-Based Marketing Division of Demonink)

Account Executive - Southwest Region

Responsible for Sales of Perfectmix Paid Search Marketing, Search Engine Optimization, and Affiliate Marketing Services targeting U.S. Companies. Primarily target C-Level executives at Fortune 500 Companies using competitive intelligence and marketing data from 3rd party resources such as: HitWise, AdGooRoo, Forrester, Yahoo!, Buzz, & Comscore.

- Increased revenue by 217%.
- Ranked #1 out of 14 Account Executives.
- Obtained new business with ABC Corporation accounting for $1.2 million in new revenue.
- ABC Corporation became Perfectmix's most profitable customer in year one.
- Obtained new business with 123 Incorporated worth an incremental $1.1 million.
- Won Circle of Excellence Trip Award.

Los Angeles Grind, Los Angeles, CA   1999 to 2006

Senior Account Executive

Responsible for the Southern California market for internet recruiting services, banner advertisements, and multi media campaigns for Fortune 500 and 1000 companies. Client target list includes Boeing, Mitsubishi, Healthnet, Northrop Grumman, Corinthian Colleges, and Ameriquest. Launched Careerbuilder.com in So. California market in 1999.

- Achieved #1 Online Sales Person out of 13 in the Classifieds Division 2004.
- Exceeded yearly quota for 5 consecutive years by 128% to 165%.
- Obtained a 132% increase versus Quota in 2005.
- Awarded Los Angeles Grind's 2001 Online Sales Person of the Year.
- Successfully increased Los Angeles Grind market share to become the #1 Tribune newspaper for Careerbuilder sales for five consecutive years.
- Ranked #1 Sales Person for CalendarLive in 1999, 2000.

GoodFood.com, San Francisco, CA   1997 to 1999

Regional Sales Representative

Responsible for United States Business Development targeting the Restaurant industry in a start-up environment. Designed the sales strategy and training collateral for new markets.

- Obtained 180 new customers in year one which led to an incremental $2 million in revenue, including Dominos, Brinker International, and Patina.
- Produced #1 sales in the Region and ranked #4 out of 60 nationally in 1998.
- Built company sales force from 4 to 60 Regional Sales Representatives through a 7 member multi-functional team effort.

AFTER

Pat Peoples

Equiscam International, Inc., Las Vegas, NV   1995 to 1997

Sales and Marketing Representative

Primary responsibilities include managing the existing client base and developing new business in the Restaurant, Real Estate Developer, and other Commercial Businesses.

- · Ranked #3 out of 57 Sales and Marketing Representatives in the nation in 1996.
- Obtained over $1.1 million in new business with Sysco Distributors, servicing TGI Fridays, and Benningtons.

ADDITIONAL TRAINING

Careerbuilder.com Bi-annual Training Seminars, 2001-2005
Non-Manipulative Selling, 2000
SPIN Selling, 1999

EDUCATION

University of North Texas
Masters Graduate Program (completed 30 credit hours)
GPA: 3.4/4.0

Texas A&M University
BS Psychology
Cum Laude Honors; GPA: 3.3/4.0

Did you see how we cleaned up Pat's résumé, making the accomplishments hard-hitting and meaningful? We consistently used strong action words in describing accomplishments. This résumé became much clearer and more concise. Pat was thrilled with the improvements. They took Pat less than a half-hour. The result: job offer and dream job!

The following "sample" résumé is an actual one (with names changed) of a person I placed at the VP level with a Fortune 500 company.

Though I thought her résumé was a little wordy, it worked. The content of responsibilities and accomplishments was an ideal match for my client's needs. In fact, the VP of HR called me immediately after she received the combination of my write up with Sharon's résumé. She enthusiastically asked, "When can we see this candidate? She looks perfect!" I love it when that happens. And Sharon was perfect for the job. She nailed it! At the time, it was my most lucrative placement.

EXAMPLE

Sharon Revenue
123 Success Lane
Anyexit, New Jersey 08888
(908) 123-4567 (H)
(908) 123-4568 (W)

PROFESSIONAL EXPERIENCE:

PHENOMENAL PRODUCTS June 1992–Present
Liberty Corner, New Jersey

Director of Trade Marketing - Footcare Division *March 1994–Present*
Responsible for P&L management of an eight figure U.S. Trade Spending Budget and Program Development in a $258 million division. Report to the Vice President of Sales and supervise eight employees: one Trade Marketing Manager, three Regional Trade Marketing Managers, two Category Analysts, one Shelf Analyst and one Administrative Assistant. Provide strategic leadership and analytical direction to increase volume and profitability through effective Account Based Marketing.

- Through optimizing our Trade P&L, increased category growth by +8% (114% greater than total HBC) while reducing trade expenses by $663 thousand.
- Developed a Category Management initiative for the Footcare Category with a focus on item optimization. This program resulted in 188 new distributions in our top 25 customers, generating an incremental $14 million annually.
- Led a multi-functional team in the development of our annual trade and consumer plan. Our promotional effectiveness initiative is designed to increase brand equity.
- Restructured the department by hiring six of eight employees. Promoted three employees from entry level analyst positions to District Manager, Category Business Analyst and Supervisor, Shelf Analysis. Upgraded five of the eight positions to incorporate more talent and experience.

West Region Manager - Footcare *June 1992–Feb. 1994*
Responsible for $30 million in the 12 Western States from Colorado to Hawaii. Supervised 35 employees: three District Managers who managed 17 Territory Managers in our direct sales business; two Broker Managers who supervised nine Brokers and two Distributors. Directly responsible for the Safeway Corporate account.

- Achieved +19% growth in 1993 highlighted by 125% attainment of new products volume objective. Delivered a net gain of 256 new items into distribution, resulting in $2 million in incremental annual sales.
- Increased the Footcare Category by 10%, outpacing the national average by 43%.
- Ranked #1 in market share and factory sales growth in 1992 versus peer group.
- Led a major restructure in an upgrade of talent while reducing expenses by $600 thousand. Hired five employees and promoted one District Manager and two Territory Managers.
- Achieved full distribution at each Safeway Division for a major new products launch through a strategic alliance with Safeway Corporate.

The Promote and Gamble Distribution Company April 1980–April 1992

District Manager - Grocery Retail Ops *Jan. 1991–April 1992*
Responsible for over $1 billion in retail sales for the Company's Food/Beverage, Soap and Paper divisions with budgets totaling $4 million. Managed the Los Angeles District including Southern California, Arizona, and Nevada during the first full year of implementation. Responsible for a staff of 50 employees: five Unit Managers, two Market Field Managers, one Shelf Analyst, one Marketing Manager, one Administrative Assistant and 40 Sales Representatives. Personally managed the P.I.A. brokerage organization.

EXAMPLE

Sharon Revenue

- Led the integration of two formal Account Teams, three Sector Sales organizations, P.I.A. brokerage and Retail Operations. Created a strategic plan to finish among the top three Districts in the U.S. for speed of placement, display levels and shelf space gains for two major product launches.
- Achieved the highest increase in display levels (+128%) in the Laundry, Fabric Conditioner, Diaper and Juice categories which accounted for 60% of total grocery volume.
- Restructured sales territories, set new training standards and promoted two Managers and three Sales Representatives.
- Developed strategy and resource deployment model that was used in a National Training Video.

District Manager - Seattle Paper Products   *December 1985–December 1990*

Managed 23 people consisting of four Unit Managers, one District Field Representative, 16 Sales Representatives and two Administrators. Responsible for $80 million in annual sales, covering a five state area from Oregon to Alaska. Personally handled the Safeway, Seattle account.

- Ranked #1 among the five Grocery Divisions in shipment development (Safeway) for four consecutive years. Surpassed volume targets each year.
- Designed a unique promotion plan and family pack initiative that improved profits in the Tissue and Towel business six fold.
- Successfully led the District to among the top five Districts in the U.S. for achieving new product volume objectives. Was the first District in the U.S. to achieve category leadership on the Always brand.
- Trained and promoted one Unit Manager, Four District Field Representatives and seven Sales Representatives.

Unit Manager - Special Assignment   *November 1984–November 1985*

Assigned to Sales Recruiting Department with responsibility for the Western Region and support of the Company's international operation in Mexico. Trained 45 Unit Managers and District Field Representatives as well as two College Recruiting teams on interviewing, recruiting and personnel planning.

- Inherited a vacant Region with a significant backlog of training needs. Conducted 635 interviews, filled every vacancy and training need in 12 months.
- Developed P & G's World Class College Recruiting Plan that was rolled out nationally.

Unit Manager - Denver Paper Products   *December 1981–October 1984*

Managed four Sales Representatives, two part-time Merchandisers and personally handled four key accounts in the Utah and Idaho market. Personal accounts were Albertsons, Smiths, Safeway and Associated Foods. Annual sales responsibility of $25 million.

- Ranked #1 in the Western Division. Only Unit in the West to exceed sales quota every year.
- Obtained new distribution on 100% of opportunities on established brands.
- Developed and promoted three Sales Representatives to District Field Representative.

Sales Representative - Los Angeles Paper Products   *April 1980–Nov. 1981*

Managed a retail sales territory in North San Diego area consisting of 150 retail accounts with annual volume of $1.4 million. Spent last two months assigned to the District Manager doing special project work including training new Sales Reps, College Recruiting and Safeway Division headquarter work.

EDUCATION:

GREATEST UNIVERSITY
B.S. - Business Administration
G.P.A. 3.5/4.0

EXAMPLE

Sharon Revenue

Starting Goalie for Field Hockey Club Team.

Special Olympics Volunteer.

Paid for college education by working throughout academic year and summers.

PROFESSIONAL AFFILIATIONS:

- Guest contributor to Category Management Seminar sponsored by the Institute for International Research in 1995.
- Los Angeles Corporate Coordinator for Inroads, a non-profit organization for minority students and the business community.
- Attended Steven Covey Principle Centered Leadership Seminar.

PERSONAL:

Married, 2 children.

Have you seen enough sample résumés yet? I hope the before and after examples were compelling and made you want to take another look at your résumé. I will end this important section with a practical template to use as you make over your own résumé. It really is easy to follow and takes away any of your résumé phobias:

TEMPLATE

Your Name
(use the first name you want to be called)
Address
City, State & Zip Code
Phone Number

Professional Experience:

Company XYZ   Month, Year - Present
(if it's a well known company, use bold, block letters; if not, italicize)

Current Job Title   Month, Year - Present
(if not impressive/applicable: don't bold but italicize; if impressive, no italics and bold)

In three sentences in this paragraph form, describe what you do. Use font size 12 and "full justify"; list your responsibilities: the scope of your responsibilities; the industry you are in; your basic products/services; revenue size if over $1 million; people you manage directly and indirectly by title (Titles are always capitalized).

- Accomplishments in bullet format—five is about the right number, starting with your greatest and most applicable to your dream job and dream company.
- The more you quantify and qualify each bullet point, the more believable—and impressive—they become.
- Revenue growth should be double digits.
- Specific accomplishments with customers (who are important to your target dream company) are very effective.
- Awards, ranking #1 vs. peer group, promoting employees due to your development of them, being selected by senior management to improve operations/save time.

Next Job Title   Month, Year—end Month, Year
Follow the same format here as before.

Next Job Title   Month, Year—end Month, Year
Follow the same format here as before.

TEMPLATE

Your Name—2

(Important to label each page since they are usually printed—make it idiot proof, so the interviewer doesn't fumble and get your résumé mixed with someone else's.)

Additional Training

List all applicable training you have received by title and date.

You can include training provided by your company or outside agencies.

If you can throw in Harvard, Steven Covey (impressive name dropping) all the better.

You can list proficiencies with software if desired by target dream company (PowerPoint, Excel, Word and others).

Education

College Name (bold if impressive; if not, italicize it)   Year started—Year finished
Degree   (if in 4 years, otherwise, just list graduation year)

GPA (if over a 3.0 out of 4.0 scale—list it; if it's not listed, they assume you have the John Belushi GPA)
Honors (Magna, Summa or Cum Laude if you can)
Financed 100% of education through part-time work and/or scholarship (list if over 50 percent—it shows you can multi-task)

Personal

Married, Number of Children (In most companies, this shows stability and paints you as desirable. If you are female, this is very beneficial—most employers will wonder if you will quit and become a stay-at-home mom after your first child? List number of children and it takes you over the hurdle.)

More Résumé No-Nos

Do not say, "References Available on Request." It says *blah, blah, blah* and it's assumed.

Don't list a bunch of unrelated hobbies. Triathlons are impressive at the gym, but listing them on your résumé will make an employer wonder when you will have time to do this job if you are working out eight hours per day. The same goes for listing golf, mountain biking, skydiving, and other time-consuming activities. And don't put "enjoy spending time with family" either.

Don't list religious or political affiliations, unless you know it is a benefit to everyone who may interview you at your target dream company. Talking religion and politics is a "no-no" during an interview, so don't invite the interviewer to give you the "heave-ho" before you even meet.

Keep the smallest font size at 12. Don't be tempted by the prospect of fitting your entire résumé on one page or even two pages. Remember, on résumés, size doesn't matter (had to throw it in again). What matters is content. Ask yourself, "Does my résumé provide my responsibilities and what I have accomplished?"

Don't rely solely on spell-check. Spell-check allowed me to be a *Manger* instead of a *Manager*—and I was applying for a Sales Manager's job—not a Nativity Scene Engineer's job. Reread and have others read and reread every word.

Now, you're ready for the final litmus test. Place your original résumé on your desk next to your new, improved version. Ask yourself which one looks like the person making the most money? If you answered the new one, give yourself a pat on the back and get ready to "get the word out" with your marketing strategy.

I am forever grateful and connected to the following pieces of wisdom I have been lucky enough to read, listen to, and watch. Although this is not the complete list, the following have had a profound effect and influence on me.

Mystical Books

Abraham DVD Series by Esther and Jerry Hicks

Ask and It Is Given by Esther and Jerry Hicks

The Bible

Buddha—A Story of Enlightenment by Deepak Chopra

Burt Goldman Mindbox CD Series by Burt Goldman

Chicken Soup for the Soul by Jack Canfield and Mark Victor Hansen

Conversations with God by Neale Donald Walsch

Don't Sweat the Small Stuff by Richard Carlson, PhD

Energy Medicine by Donna Eden

The Eye of the I by David Hawkins, MD, PhD

The Genie Within by Harry Carpenter

The Heart of the Buddha's Teaching by Thich Nhat Hanh

The Hidden Messages in Water by Dr. Masaru Emoto

How Full Is Your Bucket? by Tom Rath and Donald O. Clifton, PhD

Inner Skiing by Timothy Gallwey

Inner Tennis by Timothy Gallwey

Jose Silva Mind Control CDs—9 CD set by Jose Silva

Jose Silva's Everyday ESP by Jose Silva, Jr.

The Law of Attraction by Esther and Jerry Hicks

The Law of Attraction in Action DVD by Esther and Jerry Hicks

Mark Twain's Helpful Hints for Good Living by Mark Twain

Mars and Venus Diet and Exercise Solution by John Gray

Mission by Mark Link, SJ

A New Earth by Eckhart Tolle

Order Out of Chaos by Ilya Prigogine

The Passion Test by Janet Bray Attwood and Chris Attwood

The Pendulum Kit by Sig Lonegren

The Power of Now by Eckhart Tolle

Power vs. Force by David Hawkins, MD, PhD

Psycho Cybernetics by Dr. Maxwell Maltz

Quantum Reality: Beyond the New Physics by Nick Herbert

The Quantum World: Quantum Physics for Everyone by Kenneth Ford

Seasons of the Spirit by Sally Coleman and Maria Porter

The Secret DVD and book (both the same content) by Rhonda Byrne

The Sedona Method by Hale Dwoskin

Self Mastery Through Conscious Autosuggestion by Emile Coue

Seth Speaks by Jane Roberts

The Silva Mind Control Method by Jose Silva

Think and Grow Rich (original 1937 version) by Napoleon Hill

Three Magic Words by U.S. Andersen

What The Bleep Do We Know? DVD

You the Healer by Jose Silva and Robert B. Stone

Your Body Doesn't Lie by Dr. John Diamond

Business Books

The 100 Best Companies to Work For in America by Robert Levering and Milton Moskowitz

The Art of War by Sun Tzu

The Automatic Millionaire Homeowner by David Bach

Beware the Naked Man Who Offers You His Shirt by Harvey Mackay

Career Match: Connecting Who You Are with What You'll Love to Do by Shoya Zichy

Creating and Motivating a Superior, Loyal Staff by National Institute of Business Management

The Directory of Executive Recruiters by Kennedy Publications

Getting Things Done by David Allen

Good to Great by Jim Collins

How to Sell Anything to Anybody by Joe Girard

In Search of Excellence by Tom Peters

Knock 'Em Dead by Martin Yate

Lions Don't Need to Roar by D.A. Benton

The One Minute Manager by Kenneth Blanchard, PhD, and Spencer Johnson, MD

A Passion for Excellence by Tom Peters and Nancy Austin

Peak Performers by Charles Garfield

Rites of Passage at $100,000+ by John Lucht

Success Secrets by Mark McCormack

Talk Your Way to the Top by Kevin Hogan

Think and Grow Rich (original 1937 version) by Napoleon Hill—I have to list it again!

Warren Buffett Speaks by Janet Lowe

The Warren Buffett Way by Robert Hagstrom

What They Don't Teach You at Harvard Business School by Mark McCormack

Acknowledgments

First and foremost, I am eternally grateful to God—my Creator and Co-Creator. I am astounded by the perfect universe You have created for everyone. Your joy, love, and truth leave me in constant awe.

My mother and father were both English majors in college, so I guess I was programmed and destined to "read and write." I did both. I am grateful for the inspiration that you both gave me over the years. My mother introduced me to my mystical side with the book *Inner Skiing* and so many other books afterward; my father inspired me to excel in school even when I wanted to be a "dumb jock." I could not have written *The Bliss List* without their love, support, and patience.

To M.A.H.—the love of my life. Her love, support, and guidance are truly amazing. She is my inspiration and has taught me so many beautiful lessons.

To my children: Paul, Chris, and Jackie. May you follow your bliss and inspire your children to follow their bliss.

To my clients: I couldn't have become financially independent to write this book without your business. Thank you for your confidence in me. To my candidates: One of my greatest joys is to help you find bliss in your occupations. I am a better person because of you.

To Lisa Pelto, Ellie Pelto, Erin Pankowski and Gary Withrow at Concierge Marketing and Sandra Wendel, editor extraordinaire. This book would not be possible without you.

Special thanks to Elaine Johnson, my favorite grammarian; Bob Condello for your creative and practical guidance; Myra, my number one fan; and Meredith, a great mentor and friend.

About the Author

J P (James Parker) Hansen was born and raised in Madison, Wisconsin. He attended Boston College, where he studied English and Economics. Following college, he ascended corporate ladders at blue-chip companies: Nestle, Bristol-Myers Squibb, SC Johnson Wax, and ConAgra. In 1994, he founded Hansen Executive Search, Inc., and is currently its President. Though the corporation has earned millions of dollars, he is most proud of the fact that he has helped thousands of people find bliss in their dream jobs.

Visit www.YourBlissList.com.

Index

Writing down your goals and aspirations is the first step you can take in actually accomplishing them. *The Bliss List Journal* provides a useful and easy way to document your Bliss Lists, Bliss Cards, Bliss Boards and more.

With *The Bliss List Journal*, featuring JP Hansen's Six Spokes of Bliss, you'll discover insightful and entertaining facts on your way to "living the dream".

Available online at www.YourBlissList.com!

Exploring
Galveston

A NATURALIST'S GUIDE TO THE ISLAND

By Steve K. Alexander

Edited by Melissa Weber
Designed by Jan Pults

Printed in the United States of America

Proceeds from the sale of this book will benefit the Sea Camp Scholarship Fund at Texas A&M University at Galveston. Sea Camp is a weeklong summer camp that provides hands-on marine adventures to children ages 10 to 18.

First edition

Library of Congress Control Number: 2017904803

ISBN 978-0-692-86343-5

Stories were previously published by *The Galveston County Daily News*. Photos are by the author unless otherwise noted. Map of the upper Texas coast copyright © 2007 by John B. Anderson.

TO MY FAMILY —

Pam, Steve Jr. and Melissa, who have joined me on many coastal explorations and who keep my flame alive,

and

Paul III, who already outshines his grandpa and will likely be the future naturalist in the family.

Dr. Sammy Ray,
or as Sea Campers
called him, Papa Smurf.

(Photo courtesy of Daisy Dailey,
Sea Camp director)

IN MEMORY OF

Dr. Sammy Ray, Emeritus Professor at Texas A&M University at Galveston, who died Oct. 14, 2013, at age 94.

Dr. Ray was a world-renowned marine scientist and a founder of Texas A&M University at Galveston. He served as a mentor and role model to many marine biologists throughout his long career. The author is one.

To honor Dr. Ray's memory, proceeds from the sale of this book will be donated to the Sea Camp Scholarship Fund. Sea Camp is a weeklong summer camp at Texas A&M University at Galveston that provides hands-on marine adventures to children ages 10 to 18. Dr. Ray founded the program in 1986. The camp has so far introduced the marine environment to more than 24,000 children.

"Not all those who wander are lost."

—From the poem "All That Is Gold Does Not Glitter" by J.R.R. Tolkien in *The Lord of the Rings*

CONTENTS

Laffite's Cove Nature Preserve

Paved paths wind through the Laffite's Cove Nature Preserve on Galveston's west end.

the good side of seaweed

Photo by: JENNIFER M. PADILLA/The Daily

Camden Celis, 2, watches his family and friends in the surf at Stewart Beach on May 11. The toddler refused to walk through the seaweed covering the beach. Despite beachgoers' protests to sargassum, it actually provides an important part of the ecosystem.

Sargassum an integral part of ecosystem

Saving room for nature

Laffite's Cove Nature Preserve is a gem

A Texas Spiny Lizard scurries up a tree.

Guest column

Steve Alexander, a retired marine scientist, is a Texas Master Naturalist and an adjunct faculty member at Texas A&M University at Galveston. He's a regular contributor to The Daily News.

Along Galveston's West Bay are canal communities made of long rows of houses all along man-made canals. They're all similar except one, where houses are built only along the edges of maps, uninterrupted swaths of open, Laffite's Cove Nature Preserve.

This seemingly misplaced landscape is there because of a lawsuit brought by landowners and environmental groups against Mitchell Development Corp., and its 1974 bid to develop what is now known as Laffite's Cove.

As part of the eventual settlement, 32 untouched acres were set aside and the houses and canals were built around it.

The natural parcel of land is to be kept in perpetuity as a public place for the quiet enjoyment of nature.

In 1992, its management passed to the newly formed Laffite's Cove Nature Soci-

See Alexander | B8

ABOVE: A boardwalk crosses through the wetlands at Laffite's Cove Nature Preserve to the wooded area, popular with bird enthusiasts. **BELOW:** A blue jay perches in the woods.

A trip to Galveston's western edge reveals...

Sea OF sand

Sand ranns freely along the San Luis Pass

ABOVE: A Texas birding trail sign marks the entrance to The Gulps Woods Nature Sanctuary at state Highway 361 off Andy Road in Galveston. **BELOW:** A deer gathers pollen from a prickly pear cactus bloom in the sanctuary.

A refreshing BEAK WALK

Naturalist celebrates 60th birthday in unusual way

Story and photos by STEVE ALEXANDER • Special to The Daily News

Nautical charms

Discover treasures in a tour near The Strand

Rebuilding dur
nature's u

Galveston Island's beachfront slowly returning to

In 2008, Hurricane Ike destroyed most of Galveston Island's beachfront dunes, its primary line of defense against storm waves and surge.

Soon after Ike, beachfront homeowners rebuilt dunes lost in front of their property. Workers used machines to deposit countless loads of sand on the upper beach, where dunes were sculpted into walls and planted with sea oats and marsh hay. Nature has moved in. It took a year before the area was even visible, but before dunes even began to take their pre-Ike form.

PREFACE

MY FAMILY MOVED TO GALVESTON ISLAND when I was 9 years old. But my first memories of the beach are from high school. That's when I became a surfer.

Walter, my best friend at the time, had an older brother, Bert, who rented surfboards on the beach at 37th Street. Walter and I hung out at the beach and occasionally helped Bert by wading out to tell people their rental time was up. In return, he let us ride surfboards for free when crowds thinned late in the day.

Despite my best efforts, I never became a very good surfer. Walter, however, was pretty good. He placed in one of the local surfing contests we both entered. I didn't.

Galveston Island's bay side wasn't at all on my radar until I attended the University of Houston. It was then that I took a marine biology course from Dr. Nick Fotheringham, a professor who received his doctorate from the Scripps Institute of Oceanography in California, one of the world's foremost oceanographic institutes.

One of the course requirements was an independent study on a marine animal. I picked the moon snail as my subject, deciding to examine how the snail expands its massive foot. I collected snails on walks along salt marsh-lined bay shorelines. It was my introduction to a world beyond the sand and surf.

As a graduate student at Louisiana State University in Baton Rouge, I discovered my first love: coastal wetlands. I took frequent field trips down to the salt marshes of Barataria Bay. An image from those days still stays with me: the sight of nothing but salt marshes in all directions.

My professional career began at Texas A&M University at Galveston, where I spent a decade teaching field-oriented courses like Marine Ecology and doing oil spill research in salt marshes.

I then spent nearly two decades at the University of Mary Hardin-Baylor in Belton, Texas, where my favorite courses – Invertebrate Zoology and Field Expedition to the Texas Coast – allowed me to take students into the field in Port Aransas, Texas.

I'm now back at Texas A&M University at Galveston as an adjunct professor, teaching Coastal Wetlands Management. I also volunteer as a Texas Master Naturalist, having so far spent more than 2,500 hours taking Galveston visitors on beach and bay walks, patrolling beaches for nesting sea turtles and managing the island's Lafitte's Cove Nature Preserve.

The stories in this book – the result of decades spent wandering Galveston Island and Bolivar Peninsula – were previously published by *The Galveston County Daily News* as part of a nature series. I thank Heber Taylor, former editor of the *Daily News*, for his support and encouragement over the seven years that I contributed to the newspaper. I also thank Michael Smith, the paper's current editor.

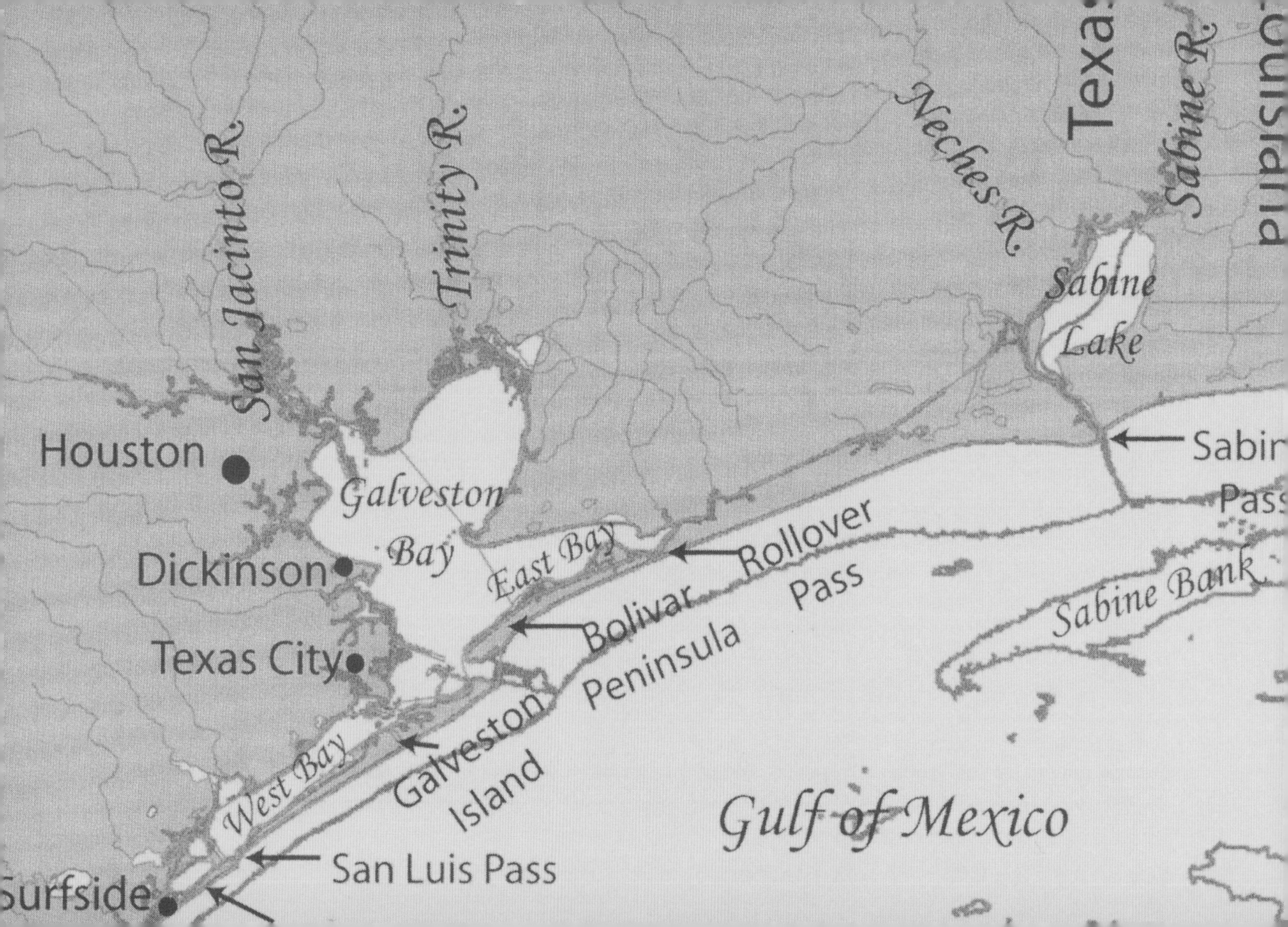
San Jacinto R.
Trinity R.
Neches R.
Texas
Sabine R.
Louisiana
Sabine Lake
Houston
Galveston Bay
Dickinson
East Bay
Texas City
Sabine Pass
Rollover Pass
Bolivar Peninsula
Sabine Bank
Galveston Island
West Bay
San Luis Pass
Surfside
Gulf of Mexico

THIS BOOK OFFERS a unique look at the best of what a 55-mile stretch of the upper Texas coast has to offer, from San Luis Pass on the western edge of Galveston Island to High Island, just east of Rollover Pass on Bolivar Peninsula.

The entire Texas coastline stretches 367 miles, from southernmost Brownsville to northernmost Sabine Lake. Barrier islands that front shallow bays, such as Galveston Bay, characterize the coastline.

The natural habitats of Galveston and other barrier islands include sandy beaches, swales, coastal prairies, potholes, salt marshes, mudflats and seagrass beds. Sandy beaches and dunes face the constant waves of the Gulf of Mexico on the front side of a barrier island, while an island's back faces calm, shallow bays occupied by salt marshes and mudflats.

Coastal prairies – a mixture of grasses and herbaceous flowering plants – fill the space between these two habitats. Depressions that hold rainwater are a type of freshwater wetland called a pothole if located in the prairie, while those located behind beachside dunes are called a swale.

The stories in this book take you to Galveston's fascinating natural habitats, from the beach and wetlands to the nature preserves. You'll also find that some of Galveston's premier tourist attractions have their own natural wonders.

The stories about Bolivar Peninsula include a lighthouse, a world-class birding destination called Bolivar Flats, a view of High Island's water bird rookery and a look at the recovery of the peninsula's beaches after Hurricane Ike devastated the area in 2008.

I take a camera wherever I go, so you'll see it all.

And when you set out on your own adventure, make sure to look closely at all the things that might otherwise go unnoticed.

< *Galveston Island and Bolivar Peninsula front Galveston Bay on the upper Texas coast. (Map courtesy of John B. Anderson)*

< *Waves break on the Galveston Island shoreline.*

Sea & Shore

Chapter 1

< Tall sand dunes form the backdrop of the shore at San Luis Pass.

A sea of sand

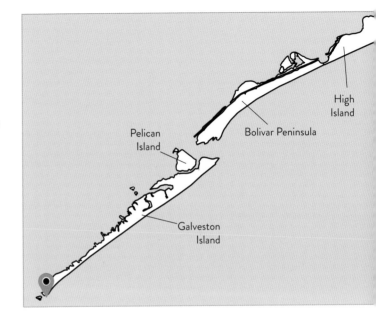

A T THE WESTERN END OF GALVESTON ISLAND lies a 1.5-mile elevated bridge that crosses San Luis Pass to reach San Luis Island.

Westbound travelers leaving Galveston view a sand panorama that stretches from the beach on their left to the bay on their right, an area of almost 400 acres. But the view allows only fleeting glimpses through a car window. To get a better look, I walked the terrain from beach to bay.

The three-hour walk revealed an important detail I'd missed on trips traversing the bridge: The westernmost end of Galveston is not only draped in sand, but the sandy beachfront extends seaward almost three football fields. The average Galveston beach, by comparison, is barely long enough for a short punt.

On this remote end of the island, sand is everywhere. Large dunes form the tall backdrop for the sandy shore. Large mounds of sand accumulate around bridge support columns. And immense sand flats stretch into the distance just inside the pass.

So where does all this sand come from? From Galveston itself. Along the island's entire length, sand is transported westward by a natural process called the longshore current.

This westward movement occurs at the astounding rate of one dump-truck load of sand every 20 minutes, wrote marine geologist John B. Anderson in *The Formation and Future of the Upper Texas Coast.*

The result: This western edge serves as the sand repository of Galveston Island.

San Luis Pass is one of only two passes along the entire Texas coast that has not been altered or modified for navigation. This leaves sand arriving at the western edge to roam freely.

Then, the force of waves, winds, currents and occasional storms begin to work, molding a sand masterpiece.

Sometimes, waves and winds capture the tiny grains before they reach the pass. Blown shoreward, they're sculpted into dunes.

THIS WESTWARD MOVEMENT OCCURS AT THE ASTOUNDING RATE OF ONE DUMP-TRUCK LOAD OF SAND EVERY 20 MINUTES.

At its widest point, you can walk nearly 1,000 feet inland from the water's edge before reaching loosely piled ridges at the base of the dunes.

From these ridges, dunes continue landward up to 300 feet and rise to heights of 10 feet. Sand arrives quickly on the dunes, proven by the half-buried stems of beach panic grass.

Windblown sand not trapped by dunes blows shoreward, where it is trapped by bridge support columns. Mounds of sand hug the columns and reach up toward the roadway.

Sand that escapes the waves and winds at the western edge continues toward the pass and is carried onward by longshore currents.

Once in the pass, longshore currents hand off the sand to tidal currents that sweep it into the bay. Tidal currents are created by flooding tides, which carry tremendous volumes of water into the bay, enough to raise water levels a foot in just hours. These currents are extremely dangerous, so you'll have to look elsewhere for a good swimming hole.

San Luis Pass is a popular place for fishing but a dangerous place for swimming because of its swift tidal currents. In August 2017, Brazoria County banned swimming and wade fishing at San Luis Pass. >

Flooding tidal currents cut deep into the sand, as shown on Google Earth. A deep and wide channel has been cut at the opening to the pass. It then branches into multiple channels, each spreading out like roots of a tree.

As flooding tides carry water into the bay, currents weaken as water spreads out through multiple channels, eventually slowing enough along channel edges to allow sand to escape and drop to the bottom.

These deposits along the channel edges form extensive sand flats, a feature geologists like Anderson call a flood tidal delta.

From the shoreline, these flats are clearly visible at low tide when looking bayward. The one nearest shore extends out into the bay for hundreds of yards before it meets a distant channel. From there, another flat spreads into the distance.

These bayside sand flats teem with thousands of birds at low tide, most too far away to identify except for the large, distinctive white and brown pelicans.

As I walked to my truck after completing my look-around, I realized this world of sand is the only one of its kind on Galveston Island. Nowhere else does sand gather and roam like this.

Many make the 20-mile drive westward beyond the seawall to hike, bird watch, sunbathe and fish. Glad I joined them.

–"A trip to Galveston's western edge reveals ... sea of sand" published January 4, 2012

Extensive sand flats stretch bayward into the distance at San Luis Pass. >

< *Galveston beaches are mostly deserted in winter.*

The wintery water's edge

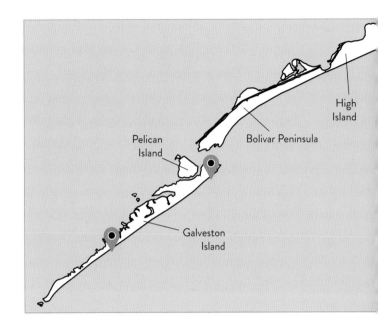

THE BEACHFRONT WAS DESERTED. No beachgoers lining the shore in a long row of chairs and umbrellas. No children building sandcastles surrounded by moats. No swimmers jumping waves in the surf.

What could explain the empty beach on a sunny, wind-free island day? Perhaps an oil spill, a red tide event or an invasion of jellyfish?

No, the explanation was much simpler than that: winter. It's the time of year when tourists head north, surrendering our beaches to the chilly air and cold water.

Without the usual drapery of people, Galveston beaches during wintertime offer a different kind of enjoyment. Imagine walking long stretches of beach in uninterrupted thought, or beachcombing when you are the only one around seeking the treasures cast ashore by waves.

While tourists abandon our beaches in winter, why should we, the locals?

Along the Texas coast, beautiful winter days aren't unusual. Mild temperatures, blue skies, calm winds, and low water levels offer a great opportunity to get out and walk a winter beach. East End or West End beaches are some of the best and most deserted beach locations on the island.

Your walk should be easier too, since winter storm waves remove much of the loose sand that piles up on the beach during summer.

On beautiful days, the inviting weather may attract a few others, but if you're lucky, you might have the beach to yourself as it stretches into the distance.

For the rugged adventurer, Galveston hasn't forgotten you. You'll have your pick of blustery winter days, with numbing cold, gusty north winds and swirling black- and gray-stained clouds. Few people, if any, venture out on such days, so absolute solitude is almost guaranteed.

For those who welcome the challenge of walking during bone-chilling, raging winds and pounding surf, you'll experience firsthand the fierce forces of nature that belly-punch the shoreline, thereby defining the nature and habits of its creatures. To survive, organisms of the shore cover up or retreat, just as a fighter would to survive another round.

Ghost crabs retreat to the safety of their deep burrows in the dunes, while the ubiquitous coquina clams, mole crabs and ghost shrimp of the swash zone cover up, digging downward to surround themselves in protective sand. Other shore creatures, such as the mobile blue crabs and speckled crabs, retreat offshore to seek the shelter of deeper water.

Winter seas are known for belching up their treasures onto the shore, so this may be the best time of year for beachcombing. Shells, sea beans, driftwood, sea glass and the rare message-in-a-bottle form a line of riches along the shore.

Whatever your preference, the wintery water's edge offers a wide assortment to choose from. And with few other beachcombers vying for treasures, you can bet your picks will be the best the sea has to offer.

If you haven't experienced the rewards of the winter beach, head out there. And do it soon, because the northern flocks of beach-loving folk will soon return.

—*"Rewards of the winter beach" published December 5, 2012*

In winter, seas toss barnacles, oysters and an assortment of seashells on to the shore.

In rough weather, coquina clams dig to bury themselves in protective sand. >

< Beach morning glory flowers are white with a yellow center

Wildflowers love the beach, too

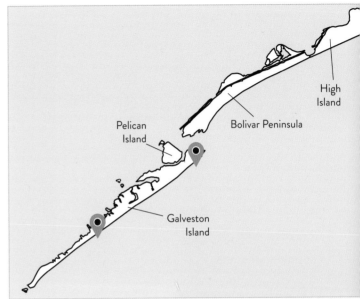

LIKE CLOCKWORK, the Texas Hill Country comes alive every spring with a colorful display of wildflowers, a palette of purples, reds, whites, yellows and pinks.

But not to be outdone, we have our own display.

While the exhibit of color to the north adorns gently sloping hillsides, ours covers upper stretches of beach, scattering a vivid mix of whites, reds, rose-purples and yellows among the drab colors of beachfront sand.

Because our beaches aren't all equally blessed with sand, it's best to visit the eastern or western ends of the island where ample sand has accumulated to support bountiful wildflowers.

In these areas, the whites of beach morning glory and yellows of beach evening primrose are the first to appear in March and April.

Morning glory white flowers are distinctive, each sporting a tubular center colored yellow. Evening primrose flowers are likewise unmistakable, each with four large yellow petals and an upward-directed four-lobed stigma. The large yellow petals appear in late afternoon or evening and then wither and turn red as they age.

Beach evening primrose flowers have four large yellow petals and a four-lobed stigma.

>

16

The lovely rose-purple flowers of railroad vine emerge a little later in the spring. Its large, uniquely shaped leaf resembles a goat's footprint and is responsible for its alternate name: goat-foot morning glory.

More than just a pretty sight, these three wildflowers are important in trapping sand and stabilizing dunes. Morning glories and railroad vines produce trailing stems, or runners, up to 100 feet long. Runners send down anchoring rootlets along their entire length, securing sand across large swathes of dunes. Although evening primroses don't form runners, they do form dense mats of vegetation that likewise hold sand in place.

∧ *Railroad vine flowers are rose-purple.*

While the three species grow on foredunes — the front side of the dunes that faces the water — sunflowers grow atop dunes. Unlike the more familiar tall sunflowers, dune sunflowers are only a foot or two tall and form a thick ground cover. But you'll still know it's a sunflower thanks to its upright flowers with yellow petals and a dark brown center.

Indian blankets also prefer dune tops. This wildflower, also called firewheel, forms a dense ground cover and produces easily recognizable flowers with yellow-tipped red petals.

Dune sunflowers are short and grow atop dunes.

>

∧ Indian blanket, also known as firewheel, produces flowers with yellow-tipped red petals.

Camphor daisy and camphorweed are wildflowers that grow closer to the water's edge on scattered piles of sand several feet high. Since both are early colonizers of these piles called coppice mounds, they are vital in trapping and holding sand along the beachfront.

The two coppice mound wildflowers are very similar, each having small yellow flowers, a short growth form and a camphor odor from crushed leaves. To distinguish them, you'll have to examine the leaf edges. If you see teeth along the leaf edges, it's camphor daisy.

These seven wildflowers are on display on our beachfront dunes each spring. Take a look soon, because when the dog days of summer arrive, the collection will be gone until next year.

—"Beach beauties: Do you know wildflowers love the beach, too?" published May 28, 2014

Teeth along the leaf edges distinguish camphor daisy (foreground) from camphorweed (background). >

< *A brown pelican (foreground) has a 7-foot wingspan.*

Brown pelicans make a big comeback

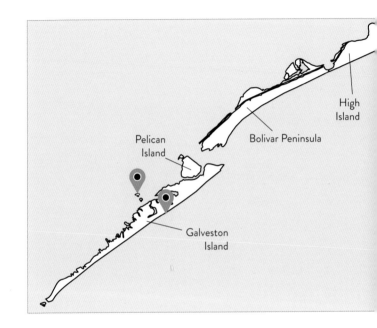

THEY'RE A COMMON SIGHT in Galveston. Their large brown bodies glide through turbulent sea breezes on the power of a 7-foot wingspan.

If you drive across the causeway or along the beachfront, chances are good you'll see some of the estimated 12,000 breeding pairs native to Texas and Louisiana.

But brown pelicans weren't always so easy to find. In the 1960s, you probably wouldn't have spotted a single pelican if you traveled across the entire 32-mile length of Galveston Island. Back then, only about 50 breeding pairs resided in all of Texas and Louisiana.

Primarily, it was the pesticide DDT that caused populations to plunge to perilously low numbers. DDT, once applied, was washed from agricultural fields into waterways, where it entered aquatic food chains.

As DDT passed through a succession of consumers, its concentration increased, reaching levels high enough in fish-eating birds to interfere with calcium deposition in the eggs.

Thin-shelled eggs, too fragile to support the weight of nesting birds, cracked when sat upon and never developed.

^ *Brown pelicans come to nest each spring on North Deer Island.*

Several federal agencies took action that subsequently aided in the recovery of the species. In 1970, the U.S. Fish and Wildlife Service provided special protection by listing the brown pelican as an endangered species. And in 1972, DDT was banned for use in the U.S. by the Environmental Protection Agency.

These actions were essential to recovery, but it was the establishment of habitats critical for breeding and raising young that allowed dwindling populations to increase.

The Audubon sanctuary on North Deer Island in Galveston Bay is one such critical habitat. This 144-acre island, with its irregular green profile of trees and shrubs, is visible from the causeway just south of the canal community of Tiki Island.

North Deer Island is one of the most important water bird nesting sites on the upper Texas coast, in the spring hosting up to 40,000 breeding pairs of 17 bird species, including brown pelicans. Thousands of adult birds come and go all day, bringing food to young birds just learning to fly.

Having witnessed the routine while on a birding tour in April 2007, I can attest to the amazing collection of sights, sounds and smells when visited up close.

From 2003 to 2007, up to 1,500 breeding pairs of brown pelicans nested each year on North Deer Island. A census in May 2011 counted more than 2,600 breeding pairs.

The recovery of the brown pelican is a welcome success story — so successful, in fact, that the brown pelican was removed from the endangered species list in 2009.

Despite healthier numbers, they continue to need our help. We must allow them to raise their families undisturbed on nesting islands, and support groups, such as the Audubon Society, that help them. Carelessly discarded fishing line or rope can entangle them, but even the most careful fisherman must keep an eye on nearby birds that might mistake their catch for an easy meal and consequently become hooked.

Galveston would have a less soulful skyline had the brown pelican not made it through tough times. As I watch them almost daily, I'm thankful for their recovery.

I'm awed by their aerial feats as they glide smoothly overhead, often in military-fashion straight lines. From 60 feet in the air, they tuck their wings and dive kamikaze-style into the water, scooping up fish in their 3-gallon pouch.

I'm envious of their aquatic ability. For them, it's a simple feat to scoop up fish between waves while swimming against choppy seas near the South Jetty. But I'm not jealous of their talents on land, as they waddle around fish markets, begging for a handout.

If they're not beachside or boat-side, they're likely keeping watch of the comings and goings across the causeway. Just outside the car window, they're the first to bid us farewell and the first to welcome us back.

—*"Making a comeback: Brown pelicans no longer in peril with thousands of breeding pairs" published August 7, 2011*

Nesting season for endangered sea turtles

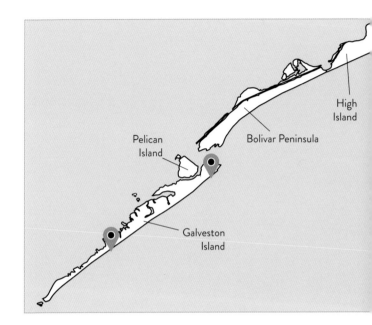

WALK THE BEACHFRONT any morning between April 1 and July 15 and you might come face-to-face with a nesting Kemp's ridley sea turtle.

It's not as much of a long shot as you might think. Just ask Jim, who in 2012 during a morning walk on East Beach, discovered a nesting sea turtle as she headed for the top of a seaweed-riddled pile of sand. Or ask Ana, whose morning stroll with girlfriends west of Jamaica Beach placed her within sight of another nester.

Jim's turtle, named Mij ("Jim" spelled backward), dug a hole in the sand-seaweed mix and laid 115 eggs. After swiping sand over the eggs and rocking back and forth to pack them, Mij, without hesitation, turned and headed back toward the water.

But before she could reach the water, several pairs of hands grabbed her and gently placed her into a padded container for transport to the NOAA Galveston Laboratory at Fort Crockett, which offers free tours available by reservation. (Visit www.galvestonlab. sefsc.noaa.gov for more information.) There, she was satellite-tagged and released some hours later.

< *An excavated nest chamber of sea turtle eggs.*

Mij transmitted data for almost a year and a half. To follow her trek through the Gulf of Mexico, visit "Track a sea turtle" at seaturtle.org.

While Mij was visiting Fort Crockett, her eggs were excavated and carefully packed in sand for transport to an incubation facility on Padre Island's National Seashore. There, her eggs were safely hatched, and the resulting hatchlings were released into the Gulf of Mexico, all in an effort to restore populations of this highly endangered species.

As for Ana, she was celebrating her birthday with family and friends when on a Saturday morning the friends set out for a walk on the beach. It was there they spotted a nesting sea turtle that was subsequently named Ana in her honor.

Ana the turtle laid eggs in a low mound of sand not far from the water. Unfortunately, the spot she chose was in the midst of a fire ant mound.

Those excavating the nest quickly became aware of this oversight. To a chorus of bites, they carefully removed her 95 eggs from the nest, wiped them clean of ants and placed them in a container of ant-free sand for transport to the Padre Island incubation facility.

Like Mij, Ana's return to the water was delayed, as she was transported to Fort Crockett for satellite tagging before release. Unfortunately, Ana transmitted data for only about a month.

Mij and Ana's nests were two of the 209 Kemp's ridley nests found along the Texas coast in 2012, a record-setting year.

When nesters begin coming ashore and you happen to see one, take note of this number to call: 1-866-TURTLE-5.

MIJ AND ANA'S NESTS WERE TWO OF THE 209 KEMP'S RIDLEY NESTS FOUND ALONG THE TEXAS COAST IN 2012, A RECORD-SETTING YEAR.

< Sea turtle tracks left behind in the sand.

Although coming face-to-face with a nesting sea turtle on the beach is a distinct possibility, there's a greater likelihood of coming across tracks nesters leave behind in the sand. That's because tracks stay on the beach much longer than do nesting sea turtles.

And tracks typically lead to a nest on the upper beach — a nest containing eggs that need to be moved for safe incubation.

Tracks are easy to spot, being about 2 feet wide with drag marks in the center and alternating check marks on each side. If you see these distinctive markings in the sand extending up the beach from water's edge, call 1-866-TURTLE-5.

A word about beachside sea turtle etiquette in case you spot a turtle or tracks: Do not attempt to corral a sea turtle or disturb her nest. Since this species is highly endangered, only permitted individuals may handle a female turtle or her eggs, according to federal law. But you are welcome to watch as permitted responders do their job.

Even without touching, just watching this nomad of the sea or witnessing excavation of their eggs is an unmatched experience you will never forget.

—"Nesting Kemp's ridley sea turtles arriving soon" published March 13, 2013

WHEN NESTERS BEGIN COMING ASHORE AND YOU HAPPEN TO SEE ONE, TAKE NOTE OF THIS NUMBER TO CALL: 1-866-TURTLE-5.

< *Sargassum stranded on the shore can create mounds several feet high.*

The good side of seaweed

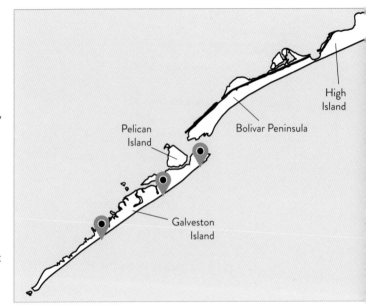

High Island

Bolivar Peninsula

Pelican
Island

Galveston
Island

LIKE CLOCKWORK, seaweed begins to blanket Texas beaches, including our own, in the spring.

Texas seaweed, commonly called gulfweed, has a more peculiar-sounding scientific name: sargassum.

Buoyed by numerous pea-sized sacs filled with air, this variety of brown algae floats in waters of the Gulf of Mexico under the influence of winds and currents. And when conditions are right, substantial amounts drift shoreward and eventually strand at the waterline.

At times, the mass of accumulating seaweed can be overwhelming, creating 2-foot-high mounds stretching for miles along the shoreline.

It's an unwelcome sight for beachgoers, who naturally prefer to walk on bare sand, rather than climb the prickly, irregular piles covering the beach. Even worse, as the piles begin to decay, they give off an offensive smell while baking in the sun.

Understandably, this ugly, stinky mess isn't why visitors delight in coming to the beach. Their simple demand: Clean it up.

In an effort to keep beach visitors happy, tourist-sustained towns like our own send out manpower and heavy equipment to haul it away. Regular cleanups continue throughout the tourist season, even when only scattered clumps wash ashore.

< *Laughing gulls wait at the water's edge to feast on the bounty of sargassum's residents.*

In 2011, seaweed washed onto Galveston beaches in unusually hefty amounts over an equally unusual period of time. Ordinarily, seaweed lands during April and May. But it began lining the shore in March and kept accumulating into June.

So, we might earlier in the year glimpse the first wave of gulfweed floating onto our beaches.

But hold that collective groan. Fact is, seaweed has a good side, ecologically speaking. It provides benefits both at sea and on shore.

At home in the Sargasso Sea and while adrift in the Gulf of Mexico, gulfweed provides a home for a community of animals similar in color and shape to the weed. These include fish, shrimp, crabs, nudibranchs, snails, worms, sea anemones, hydroids and bryozoans. And as it floats at the surface, it not only provides food and refuge for a variety of young fish, but it also is the habitat of young sea turtles.

At sea, large rafts of gulfweed, with its heap of animals, attract a variety of large predatory game fish, a tidbit well-known among seasoned offshore fishermen seeking a trophy catch.

As it washes ashore, lingering at the water's edge are laughing gulls, ring-billed gulls, sanderlings, ruddy turnstones, and willets, all waiting patiently to pick up the tiny shrimp and other resident animals dislodged from the seaweed as waves roll it across the sand.

^

A sargassum fish is one of the many residents of sargassum while adrift at sea.

34

AS IT FLOATS AT THE SURFACE, IT NOT ONLY PROVIDES FOOD AND REFUGE FOR A VARIETY OF YOUNG FISH, BUT IT ALSO IS THE HABITAT OF YOUNG SEA TURTLES.

Ghost crabs, whose burrows are typically found near the dunes, dig holes just above the water's edge among masses of stranded seaweed, a tactic that provides them easy access to a bountiful food source as it decays.

Winds and waves eventually move sargassum further up the beach, where it traps sand and attracts small invertebrates like beach fleas and flies, which in turn make a nice meal for small shorebirds. If left alone, some weed eventually migrates upward to the dunes, adding a source of nutrients that feed the growth of dune plants.

On the west end of the island, at places like Galveston Island State Park, seaweed is left on the beach to do as it will. Eventually, it's incorporated into beach sand and dunes, making these beaches up to twice as wide as those to the east and west.

One thing's for sure: It's coming. Masses of seaweed will soon cover our beaches again. But this time, maybe you'll focus less on the bad and remember the good.

—*"The good side of seaweed: Sargassum an integral part of ecosystem" published March 18, 2012*

As sargassum moves farther up the shore, it traps sand to help build the beach. >

< *Like a spider's web, amaranth's roots extend far and wide to grip the sand.*

Rebuilding dunes nature's way

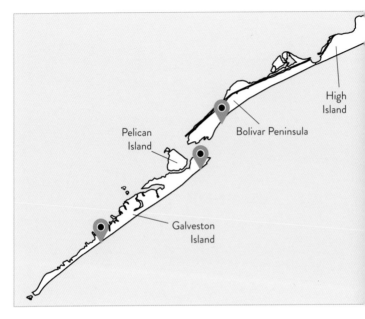

URRICANE IKE in 2008 destroyed most of Galveston Island's beachfront dunes, its primary line of defense against storm waves and surge.

Soon after Ike, beachfront homeowners rebuilt dunes lost in front of their property. Workers used machines to deposit countless loads of sand on the upper beach, where piles were sculpted into sloping walls and planted with bitter panicum and marshhay cordgrass.

Nature has moved more slowly. It took a year before nature's work was even visible, and three years before dunes even began to resemble their pre-Ike form.

I have watched the natural rebuilding of dunes at Bolivar Peninsula, East Beach and Galveston Island State Park. Nature has used winds and waves to rebuild local dunes, one grain of sand at a time.

Winds, a well-known agent of dispersal, carried plant seeds onto the beach. In the loose, dry sand on the upper beach, they germinated.

38

THESE 14 PLANT SPECIES *currently cover dune faces and coppice mounds on Bolivar Peninsula and Galveston Island.*

> Amaranth
> Beach evening primrose
> Beach morning glory
> Beach tea
> Bitter panicum
> Camphor daisy
> Coastal dropseed
> Marshhay cordgrass
> Pennywort
> Railroad vine
> Saltwort
> Sea purslane
> Sea rocket
> Western ragweed

Soon, plants sent down long roots into the sand. Beach tea sends down a single anchoring root a foot into the sand, while marshhay cordgrass secures itself using a system of long, fibrous roots.

Plants then extended roots, or rhizomes, outward to cover as large an area as possible. In amaranth, roots extend in spiderweb fashion outward to 10 feet. In marshhay cordgrass, rhizomes extend multiple feet in all directions.

Once anchored and established, plants grow upward quickly to keep from being covered with sand.

In addition to carrying seeds, winds also move water, creating the breaking waves that deliver sand to the beach.

Shoreward breezes of spring and summer carry this newly deposited sand up the beach. Tiny grains are blown shoreward by the billions, visible in high winds hugging the ground as they go, moving in waves like realms of teeming ghosts.

Without plants, the ghosts of sand would simply fly beyond the beach without stopping. But rooted plants on the upper beach form a barrier, trapping the sand against a wall of green.

Marshhay cordgrass rhizomes extend outward in all directions. >

Over time, a mound of sand and plants becomes obvious. These piles, called coppice mounds, grow in higher and wider circles, possibly joining others to form a dune line of considerable size.

This natural process is slow, still years in the making. But given time and the absence of future hurricanes pounding the Galveston shore, we'll see nature's blueprint for building dunes in her own good time.

—"Rebuilding dunes nature's way:
Galveston Island's beachfront slowly returning to pre-Ike form"
published July 3, 2011

Wind-blown sand is trapped over time by rooted plants on the upper beach, creating piles called coppice mounds. >

< Fog covers the beachfront on a winter day.

A long, long walk on the beach

WHEN I CELEBRATED my birthday in November 2009, no one knew except my wife about my plan to do something unusual to commemorate 60 years of good health and fortune.

I mentioned it to her in July when the idea first came to me. I told her I wanted to do a 60-mile beach walk, a distance twice the length of Galveston Island.

"Why a beach walk?" she asked, an odd question from her since she loves a walk on the beach as much as I do.

Despite the question, I think she already knew the answer.

For me, beach walks are great medicine. I have walked countless beaches over the years in Oregon, California, Texas, Florida, North Carolina, Maryland, New Jersey and Massachusetts.

Even though some were visited many years ago, I can still see them and I can still feel them.

44

∧ *Beach houses along the*
West End are unprotected
from future storms.

So a 60-mile beach walk seemed perfect for me. But I knew it would be a challenge and would take an estimated 25 to 30 hours.

I didn't think I could do it all at once so I planned initially to walk three days, but finally settled on walking four days.

From three seasons of sea turtle patrols, I knew I could walk 5 miles with no problem. But to do 60 miles, I knew I had to do some training.

In July, I started some serious walking but soon decided strength and endurance was what I needed, so I began going to the Racquet Club more regularly and pushing myself to lift more weight with my legs and upper body.

And all my work paid off. By mid-December, I was ready.

DAY 1

On the first day, I walked from the west end of the seawall to Jamaica Beach and back, a distance of 16 miles. The day was cool, damp and extremely foggy. Visibility most of the day was perhaps one-quarter of a mile.

Along this stretch, I saw many houses on or adjacent to the beach with no protection from future storms. They reminded me of soldiers on the front line ready to take the surge of the enemy, but without the benefit of a bunker to jump into or a wall to hunker behind.

DAY 2

I walked the entire seawall roundtrip the second day, a distance of 20 miles. The weather was cold, with strong north winds and drizzling rain.

Between 61st and 25th streets, some sand remained from the recent renourishment project, but water washed up to the seawall in places.

As I walked this stretch, I wondered how many of those who daily drive the seawall know of the art below — the dolphins, fish, sharks, rays, jellyfish, crabs, shrimp and myriad other sea creatures depicted on the front side.

At 25th Street, a pleading message in pink was added to this mix of sea creatures. It read, "Hannah ... will you marry me?"

As I continued eastward past Porretto Beach at 10th Street, the shore widened and a more expansive beach continued all the way to the South Jetty.

On Day 4, I noticed the same widening on the west end of the island. Our most expansive beaches are found at the ends, a fact probably not known by the vast majority of tourists searching for the perfect beach spot.

∧ *Fish and crabs are part of a large mural on the beach side of the seawall near 39th Street.*

^ *Sand fencing was erected in front of rebuilt dunes in an effort to trap new sand.*

Day 3 began at Jamaica Beach, then west to Terramar Beach and back, a distance of 14 miles. The day was cold but sunny.

On this stretch of beach, I was encouraged by the sight of rebuilt dunes, replanted dunes and sand fencing.

Dune reconstruction in some areas now protected entire housing developments, while in other areas rebuilt dunes were scattered here and there.

Some rebuilt dunes had been replanted while others were being colonized by volunteer plants. Sand fencing, designed to trap new sand, fronted many sections of rebuilt dunes.

This day I passed damaged multistory houses with elegant contents clearly visible through great windows. Seeing this made me realize the anxiety some of these owners must feel leaving their beachfront houses empty and unguarded after storm damage.

But I couldn't help but chuckle at the effort of one homeowner to discourage potential threats.

He posted a sign behind the dunes that read "Rattlesnake Xing." And on the wall of the house were two "No Trespassing" signs and a sign bearing the silhouette of a man with a bull's-eye in the center. It read "Nothing Inside Is Worth Dying For."

The fourth day began at Terramar Beach and then west to San Luis Pass and back, a distance covering the last 10 miles.

Near Terramar Beach, I saw a river of rainwater flowing to the Gulf. It's something I have seen on other beaches but is a rare sight on our Texas beaches.

I guess the unusually heavy rains of December had nowhere else to run except down to the beach.

Despite perfect weather and a low tide, I saw only a few beachcombers that day.

But when I got to San Luis Pass, it was lined with fishermen. From this simple observation, I must conclude that serious fishermen outnumber serious beachcombers.

Having reached my goal and feeling a sense of accomplishment, I did some beachcombing of my own on the way back.

Near the water's edge, I saw more live lettered olives — a species of sea snail known for the beauty of its shell — than I have ever seen.

— *"A refreshing beach walk: Naturalist celebrates 60th birthday in unusual way" published January 17, 2010*

∧ *Rainwater runoff formed a meandering river to the Gulf of Mexico.*

< *Immature white ibis and a willet (far left) search the salt marsh for food. (Photo courtesy of Frank Budny)*

Into the Wetlands

Chapter 2

< Smooth cordgrass grows alone at the water's edge, providing food and habitat for marsh and bay animals.

Discover the island's back side

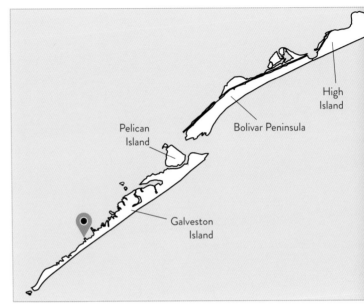

GALVESTON ISLAND HAS TWO SIDES: a front side and a back side. The front side is well-known. The back side is not.

On the island's front, waves from the Gulf of Mexico break on 30 miles of sandy beaches, from the seawall-lined eastern end to the seawall-less western end. As predictable as sunrise, when the weather warms, sandy beaches fill with people who come to walk, run, play, party, sun, read, swim, surf or fish.

On the island's back, waters of West Bay gently wash 20 miles of salt marsh wetlands, from Sportsman Road westward to San Luis Pass. When the weather warms, wetlands may host a few avid fishermen seeking trophy trout or a few birders hoping to spot a rare breed.

But the crowds never come. There are no ocean waves or wide expanses of sand. Instead, there is only quiet water, mud and grass-filled shorelines.

But the salt marsh wetlands can become better known. All that's required is a visit.

When you get out and walk around, you can better appreciate smooth cordgrass, a uniquely adapted plant whose very presence and growth provides both habitat and a source of food for numerous salt marsh and bay animals.

< *Male fiddler crabs have one large claw, while females have two small claws. (Photo courtesy of Frank Budny)*

You can see that salt marshes harbor fiddler crabs, marsh periwinkles and ribbed mussels. Bay shorelines harbor striped hermit crabs, marine worms, mud shrimp, razor clams, angel wing clams and oysters.

And when you pull a net through surrounding bay waters, you can see that this is a prime nursery area for many commercially important species, like speckled trout, redfish, flounder, black drum, croaker, brown shrimp, white shrimp and blue crabs.

∧ *Marsh periwinkles live on smooth cordgrass and periodically descend to feed on the mud surface. (Photo courtesy of Frank Budny)*

∧ *A clump of oysters clings to the shallow bay bottom, their preferred habitat.*

∧ *This striped hermit crab has chosen a lightning whelk shell to inhabit.*

*Seining bay waters adjacent to salt marsh shorelines often yields ^
a bounty of bay inhabitants.*

So, how about a visit? There is no better time than now. A guided walk at Galveston Island State Park provides a close look at salt marsh wetlands.

Called "Bay Explorations," the walk is held each March through November. Each Sunday at 10 a.m., the introduction begins at the Nature Center on the bay side of the park. Participants are led on a 1 to 1 1/2-hour walk along a bay side salt marsh. During the walk, participants see and learn about salt marsh plants and animals, bay shoreline animals, and have an opportunity to pull a net through shallow bay waters to collect the myriad swimming creatures that call this place home.

Leaders are trained volunteers, most of whom are members of the Friends of Galveston Island State Park and Texas Master Naturalists.

The "Bay Explorations" walk follows in the footsteps of the popular "Beach Exploration" walk on the beach side of the park. This program also runs from

March to November and begins at 10 a.m. each Saturday at park headquarters on the beach side of the park.

During the 1 to 1 1/2-hour walk on the beach, participants see and learn about dune plants and animals, collect shells and seaweed washed up on the shore, dig for animals in the sand and have an opportunity to pull a net through the surf.

These hands-on, field-oriented walks are available to all visitors and residents of Galveston Island for the sole purpose of educating the public about the nature and true value of our coastal habitats.

—"Get in touch with isle's back side: Discover wetlands" published March 13, 2008

The catch from bay waters often includes a variety of fish, shrimp, crabs and an occasional squid.

>

< A bullfrog hides among a mix of cattails and duckweed in a freshwater marsh.

Wetlands benefit both wildlife and people

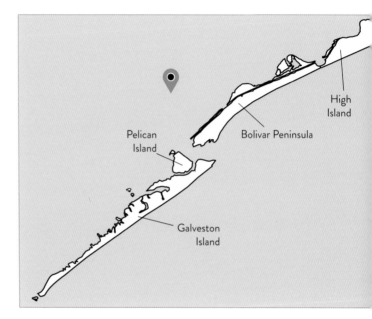

RECENTLY AFTER CLASS, one of my students stopped to ask a question about the value of wetlands, wanting more details before he presented the topic to another class. Before leaving he said, "I had no idea wetlands were so important."

His remark didn't surprise me since most people don't learn about the true significance of wetlands.

Making more people aware of the full extent of wetland values is the objective of World Wetlands Day, held each February 2. It's also the objective of this story.

Hopefully, with a greater knowledge of wetlands, more people will realize the importance of preserving, protecting and restoring these habitats.

So, what is their value?

< The American alligator is a predator typically found in fresh and brackish water marshes and swamps in southeastern states.

> PROVIDE HABITAT. Many invertebrates, fish, amphibians, reptiles, birds and mammals use wetlands during all or part of their life cycle. Blue crabs, shrimp, redfish, speckled trout, flounder, croaker, menhaden and mullet depend on Galveston Bay wetlands as habitat and nursery. Likewise, hundreds of bird species rest, eat, drink and reproduce in local wetlands.

> STORM BUFFER. Coastal wetlands function as a green wall, a barrier that lowers storm surge height as hurricanes move inland. Based on data from past hurricanes, for every 3 miles a storm travels over wetlands, storm surge height is reduced by 1 foot. Even a small reduction in the height of a storm surge can greatly reduce hurricane damage.

> FLOOD CONTROL. Wetland plants and soils take up and store water after heavy rainfalls. By holding water, they lower the amount of runoff filling streams and rivers, thus reducing the likelihood of flooding downstream.

^ *The broad-banded water snake is a resident of cypress swamps.*

^ *Black-bellied whistling ducks and their young navigate around lotus leaves in this freshwater wetland.*

60

Snowy egrets wade in the shallows of a salt marsh ∧ shoreline in search of fish.

The numerous, deeply penetrating fibrous roots of ∧ cordgrass help hold soils in place.

> SHORELINE EROSION CONTROL. Coastal wetland plants, such as cordgrass, produce a system of fibrous roots that hold soils in place. After Hurricane Ike, Galveston Island State Park's beach shoreline retreated several hundred feet, but the park's salt marsh shorelines, anchored by cordgrass roots, were unchanged.

> IMPROVE WATER QUALITY. Wetlands remove water pollutants such as heavy metals and sediment. More than 600 North American wastewater treatment plants now use wetlands as a final "polishing" step before treated wastewater is released into surrounding waterways.

> SUPPORT HIGH RATES OF PLANT PRODUCTION. Wetlands produce up to three times more plant material than cornfields. Tides and river flooding carry much of this plant material into adjacent waters where it serves as food for resident creatures.

> PLACES FOR RECREATION, EDUCATION AND WILDLIFE OBSERVATION. Because of their bountiful wildlife, wetlands offer great crabbing, fishing and waterfowl hunting. They are also ideal places to learn hands-on field biology and are hot spots for observing wildlife, especially birds.

More than half of the nation's once-existing wetlands are gone. And those losses have come with observable consequences: declines in migratory birds, declines in water quality, dead zones in the Gulf of Mexico, increased river flooding and increased hurricane damage.

Organizations such as The Nature Conservancy, Texas Parks and Wildlife, Galveston Bay Foundation, Scenic Galveston and Artist Boat are working to preserve, protect and restore wetlands.

For the rest of us, let's celebrate our local wetlands each February 2 and support all efforts to secure the future of these vitally important habitats.

—*"Wetlands have many values" published February 2, 2015*

∧ *Cattail Marsh in Beaumont, Texas, is a wastewater treatment wetland designed to "polish" treated wastewater before release.*

>
Wetlands are prime habitats for many species of birds, making them hot spots for birding.

< *After pulling the net through water, campers transfer the catch to a water-filled bucket.*

Seining along the wetlands shore

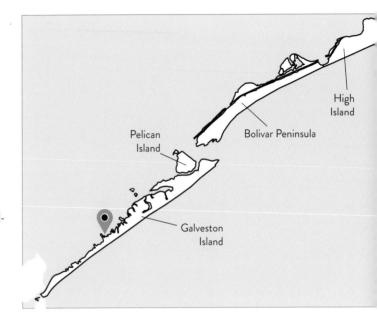

T WAS MONDAY MORNING, the first day of summer break, as I watched kids being dropped off at Galveston Island State Park for the start of Camp Wild.

There would be no beginning of the summer "brain drain" for them, because they'd spend the week fishing, crabbing, kayaking, seining, birding, beachcombing and studying wildlife.

In 2001, Mary Jean Hayden, Camp Wild coordinator, envisioned a camp that would introduce Galveston kids to the outdoor activities available in their island paradise.

The first camp had only four volunteers and 20 campers, but that Monday morning, I counted 40 volunteers and 58 kids.

I hurried to the bay side where I and a fellow Texas Master Naturalist, Nathan Veatch were to instruct kids in seining.

When the bus arrived, we watched as the kids bounded out. We met them by the r◦   ◦ed their shoes to make sure they were secure, offered life vests and then headed to the water.

Nathan and I demonstrated seining technique, being sure to tell them to shuffle their feet in case there were stingrays around. They seemed anxious at first, but within seconds, they were ready to seine.

< *A typical bay catch transferred to a water-filled viewing chamber includes anchovies, silversides and pinfish.*

Two kids — one on each end of the 20-foot net — pulled the net through the shallows for a short distance. Then everyone helped lift the net out of the water.

The catch was shaken to the center where hands picked through the webbing for flopping fish, skipping shrimp and crawling crabs.

We placed everything in a bucket and transferred the catch to viewing chambers. With the aid of these mini-aquaria, kids saw a bounty of small bay critters, including anchovies, silversides, mullet, killifish, pinfish, drum, spot, puffers, brown shrimp and blue crabs.

GALVESTON ISLAND NATURE CAMPS AND ACTIVITIES FOR KIDS

BEACH AND BAY COME OUT AND PLAY

Families can enjoy a free day of events each spring at Galveston Island State Park, courtesy of Friends of Galveston Island State Park. Activities include beach and bay nature walks, kayaking, seining, fishing and birding. fogisp.wordpress.com

CAMP WILD

A five-day camp held each June for Galveston Island students in 4th and 5th grades. Camp coordinators work with local schools to register eligible students. Parents can contact their child's school for more information.

OCEAN DISCOVERY DAY

A free day of ocean discovery is offered each spring at the NOAA Galveston Lab. Take a virtual dive, talk about dolphin rescue, learn about ocean habitats such as coral reefs, see sea turtles, and hear about marine careers.

www.flowergarden.noaa.gov

I grabbed a small blue crab and asked two boys if they wanted to experience how hard it pinched. They quickly said yes.

Each in turn held out a finger and the blue crab closed its pincher on a finger. The boys howled, quickly learning the power even in a small crab's claw. I was careful to tell them not to try this with a large blue crab, because they may not get all their finger back.

One of their favorite catches was the comb jellies, a clear jellyfish-like animal plentiful in late spring due to the abundance of plankton — their principle food source.

We pulled up hundreds of them in the net. Unafraid, the kids picked them up for closer inspection and were delighted when Nathan sneezed and seemingly expelled them from his nose.

These animals are often called sea snot, he told them. But one girl had her own name for them: goobers. At least that's what her family calls them.

ONE OF THEIR FAVORITE CATCHES WAS THE COMB JELLIES, A CLEAR JELLYFISH-LIKE ANIMAL PLENTIFUL IN LATE SPRING.

Dozens of sea nettles had washed up along the bay shoreline. I told the kids to stay clear because they deliver a very painful sting.

We also saw a moon jellyfish that measured at least a foot across — one of the biggest I have ever seen.

I managed to scoop it into a bucket so the kids could get a closer look. They watched it in the bucket as I told them about its ability to swim and capture food.

When I was done, they all wanted to take part in freeing it. An army of hands carried the bucket to shallow water where they dumped it — accidentally — upside down.

When the kids were finished with seining, they bounced off the shoreline toward the road, seemingly with as much energy as when they came.

—"There's no idle summer for kids at Camp Wild" published July 21, 2008

< *The entrance to Galveston Island State Park is located about 7 miles past the west end of Seawall Boulevard.*

GALVESTON
ISLAND
STATE PARK

Parks & Preserves

< *This view of shoreline wrack includes large amounts of seaweed and a single tree.*

A glimpse of unspoiled Galveston

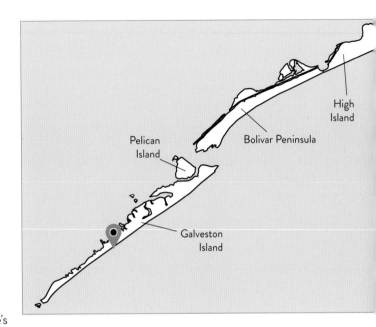

EVER WONDER what Galveston Island looked like before us land dwellers moved in? I know a place.

It's just beyond the seawall on the West End. It's Galveston in its natural state — sandy beach and dunes along the Gulf of Mexico, giving way to an interior section of coastal prairie that transforms into salt marsh and shallow bay on the back side of the island.

Such is the sequence of habitats crossing Galveston and other barrier islands that, together, form a chain along the 367-mile Texas coastline. These islands protect what's on the other side: a series of shallow coastal bays. There's Padre Island shielding the Laguna Madre at the southernmost end of the chain and Galveston Island fronting Galveston Bay at the northernmost end.

Some barrier islands along the Texas coast, like Matagorda Island just north of Port Aransas, still are completely undeveloped and display the habitat sequence in its natural state.

But Galveston is not without its natural parcels. Drive west, just beyond the seawall, to Galveston Island State Park.

< Bitter panicum's spreading growth, depicted here, traps windblown sand.

BEACHSIDE

A good place to start is on the Gulf side. Park east of the headquarters' building and take the wooden walkway to the beach. Standing on the upper beach, you'll see some of the 10,000 or so waves that break on the shore each day.

The constant action stirs the water, keeping fine mud particles in suspension, allowing only heavier sand particles to drop out. It's these sand particles that eventually move up the shore to form the beach.

You might walk along the wrack line — the part of the shore that accumulates tossed-up debris. Contributions vary from day to day, but both land and sea contribute, from the sea's plentiful seaweed to the land's copious amounts of tree trunks and limbs carried by river runoff into the Gulf.

∧ *Plants aid the slow development of beachfront dunes such as this one at Galveston Island State Park.*

74

Along the upper shore, you'll see plants such as amaranth, beach morning glory, beach tea and bitter panicum all working together to trap windblown sand to form the dunes that rise up behind you.

The dunes are critical for both beach-based animals, such as ghost crabs, and sea-based animals, such as sea turtles that come onshore to nest.

Back along the boardwalk, a large rainwater-filled depression hides within the dunes. Called a swale, this pool of water serves as nature's drinking fountain for birds and mammals.

Ghost crabs, permanent residents of beach dunes, retreat to their burrows ∧
when not out foraging for food.

Beachside swales are an important source of drinking water for island birds and mammals. >

< *A pothole wetland, one of many that dot the park's interior, serves as both a water source and habitat for wildlife.*

BAYSIDE

Across FM 3005, you can park at the Nature Center adjacent to the wind turbine. You've now entered the coastal prairie. Walk the 0.2-mile Duck Lake Trail that winds through the flat terrain and passes one of the rainwater-filled pothole wetlands that dot the park's interior.

Along the trail, there's a mix of prairie grasses, yellow coreopsis and shrubs called marsh elder. Cattle once grazed these shrubs, which now grow so tall that they must be mowed or burned to control their height. There often are signs of rodents, raccoons, coyotes or snakes along the trail and circling raptors overhead.

Finally, there's the salt marsh and shallow bay ecosystem. These wet habitats nourish the richest abundance and variety of species, many of which are sought commercially and recreationally. For a good look, walk the half-mile Clapper Rail Trail or the path at water's edge along Lake Como.

∧ *Coreopsis is one of the park's springtime wildflowers.*

Calm water prevails along these bay shores, away from high-energy waves of the beach. Fine mud particles can freely settle, forming the soft, muddy bottoms characteristic of the bay.

High tides flood the shoreline daily, allowing tall stalks of smooth cordgrass to colonize these muddy bay bottoms. With its sophisticated roots, smooth cordgrass is unique in its ability to reach out from the shore into water-saturated mud. That also means it grows alone at the bay's edge.

While an extensive system of cordgrass roots anchor mud in place below, its stems and leaves provide a dense layer of green above, a layer that provides both cover and nourishment for a vast collection of bay creatures, including fiddler crabs, periwinkle snails, ribbed mussels, juvenile fish and shrimp, hermit crabs and blue crabs.

Smooth cordgrass grows alone at the bay's edge because of ∧ its unique ability to grow in seawater-saturated mud.

Ribbonlike shoal grass is the most common sea grass in the park. It grows in shallow bay bottoms bathed in nutrient-rich water and sunlight. Their roots secure the seabed soil while green shoots provide attachment sites and refuge for micro-inhabitants that attract small predatory fish and invertebrates, which, in turn, attract larger game fish.

As an added benefit, both smooth cordgrass and shoal grass provide an ongoing supply of decaying plant material that is incorporated into shallow bay sediments. This "detritus" food material nourishes the small invertebrate animals that larger fish and birds depend on.

Galveston Island State Park remains one of the few places where you can see what the island once looked like. Such a treasure is worthy of exploration.

—"Unspoiled Galveston: A biologist looks at the state park"
published May 2, 2012

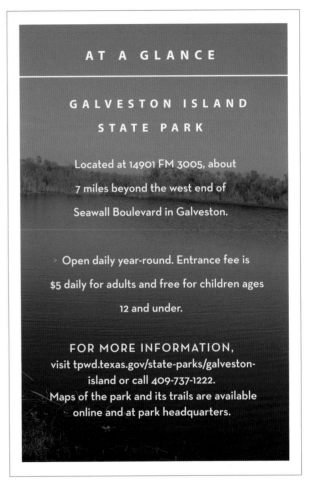

AT A GLANCE

GALVESTON ISLAND
STATE PARK

Located at 14901 FM 3005, about
7 miles beyond the west end of
Seawall Boulevard in Galveston.

> Open daily year-round. Entrance fee is
$5 daily for adults and free for children ages
12 and under.

FOR MORE INFORMATION,
visit tpwd.texas.gov/state-parks/galveston-
island or call 409-737-1222.
Maps of the park and its trails are available
online and at park headquarters.

< Seawolf Park offers unique views of Bolivar Roads ship traffic.

A park with a colorful history

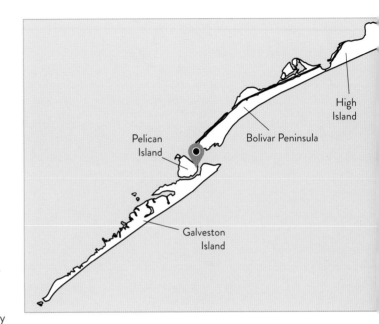

A COUGH OR SNEEZE by a visitor to Seawolf Park nowadays would expectedly go unnoticed. Not so a century ago.

Back then, the grounds of Seawolf Park, just north of Galveston Island, served as the site of the Pelican Island Federal Quarantine Station. During its 35 years of operation, an estimated 750,000 immigrants and 30,000 ships entering the U.S. were carefully examined for any signs of contagious disease.

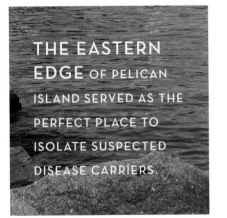

THE EASTERN EDGE OF PELICAN ISLAND SERVED AS THE PERFECT PLACE TO ISOLATE SUSPECTED DISEASE CARRIERS.

The eastern edge of Pelican Island served as the perfect place to isolate suspected disease carriers. It was remote, surrounded by water and, back then, without a bridge.

Closed in 1950 thanks to advances in disease prevention and treatment, the 10-building facility and surrounding grounds suffered years of neglect. That is until the City of Galveston acquired the property and reopened it to the public as Seawolf Park.

The T-head pier extends more than 400 feet into the bay and is one of the best fishing spots in the area.

Those who were quarantined here in the early 1900s enjoyed the shade of screened-in porches and scattered palms. Today's crowds find shade under tall palms that still dot the site and from picnic shelters, canopies and wide umbrellas. All provide a cool spot for picnicking and watching the ferry boats and ships pass through the Galveston Ship Channel and Bolivar Roads.

The park is also a fisherman's oasis. The entire shoreline is accessible, allowing many to seek the speckled trout, flounder and croaker plentiful in the surrounding open waters of the bay.

You'll often find delighted fishermen along the lighted T-head fishing pier that juts out more than 400 feet into the bay, catching the speckled trout that roam there at night.

The three-story pavilion prominently displayed on the northern tip of the park remains unusable, still open and broken, a victim of Hurricane Ike's unmerciful beating in 2008. For safety, a cyclone fence surrounds it. (The pavilion still has not been repaired as of summer 2017.)

At the southern end of the park are the USS Cavalla, a World War II submarine, and the USS Stewart, a World War II destroyer escort, one of only three left. Both are open to the public for self-guided tours.

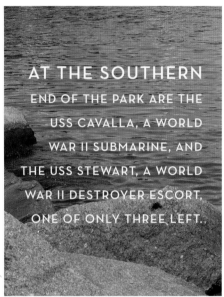

AT THE SOUTHERN END OF THE PARK ARE THE USS CAVALLA, A WORLD WAR II SUBMARINE, AND THE USS STEWART, A WORLD WAR II DESTROYER ESCORT, ONE OF ONLY THREE LEFT.

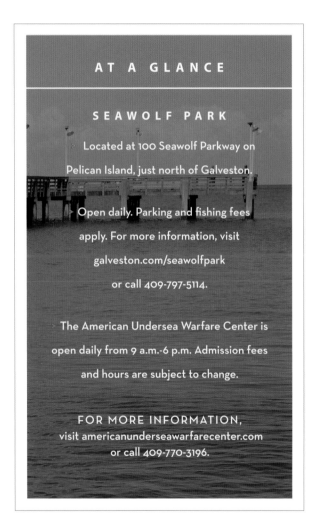

The ships are located in the park's Memorial Plaza, a place honoring veterans and service members. It's a fitting place to hold a Memorial Day observance, a fact recognized by local veterans who organize a service there each year.

Once an ideal site for isolating suspected disease carriers, the eastern edge of Pelican Island is now one of Galveston's largest recreation areas — a unique spot to take a walk through wartime naval history, to reel in a nice catch, or to picnic amid cool sea breezes, all while watching the busy scenes of surrounding waterways.

—"Seawolf Park: Keeping an eye on the past while looking to the future" published August 14, 2013

Seawolf Park's Memorial Plaza, featuring the USS Stewart (left) and USS Cavalla (right), honors veterans and service members. >

< *A red-eared turtle is a common freshwater inhabitant seen in ponds and swales.*

Saving room for nature

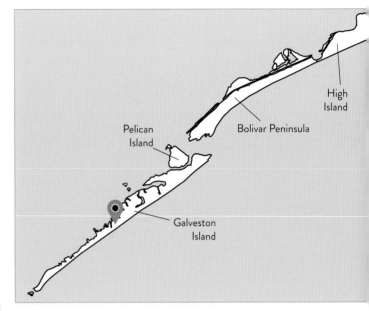

ALONG GALVESTON'S WEST BAY are canal communities made up of long rows of houses built along man-made canals. They're all similar except for one, where houses are found only along the edges of a large, uninterrupted swath of green: Lafitte's Cove Nature Preserve.

This seemingly misplaced landscape is there because of a lawsuit brought by landowners and environmental groups against Mitchell Development Corporation and its 1974 plan to develop what is now known as Lafitte's Cove. As part of the eventual settlement, 32 untouched acres were set aside and the houses and canals were built around it.

This natural parcel of land was to be kept in perpetuity as a public place for the quiet enjoyment of nature.

In 1992, its management fell to the newly formed Lafitte's Cove Nature Society. Their job has been to protect and maintain the area as a freshwater ecosystem.

Today, the land set aside decades ago still supports a freshwater swale and its surrounding ponds, shrub thickets, wooded forests and grasslands — all surrounded by two- and three-story houses.

< *The elevated boardwalk provides a close-up view of bulrushes and cattails, and sometimes red-eared turtles and nutria.*

Contained within the preserve is a respectable assemblage of freshwater biota, including whistling ducks, blue-winged teal, mockingbirds, white ibises, red-eared turtles, cattails, bulrushes, spike rushes and sedges.

Added to these are resident woodland species and transient bird populations that use woodlands during spring and fall migrations.

An elevated boardwalk begins at the parking lot, providing a close-up view of the freshwater swale. Tall bulrushes and cattails grow within arm's reach and water hyssop covers much of the mud surface below.

When the swale fills with rainwater, the critters that blossom in mud and water attract wading birds such as white ibis.

∧ *Redheads, a winter visitor to the island, form a duck armada in one of the ponds.*

A layer of duckweed-dominated green covers this ^
bulrush-lined freshwater swale.

Beyond the boardwalk is a path to the gazebo, a place providing a view of one of the ponds. From here, a trail leads into the woods. Several water drips along the pathway fill pools with cool, clear water sure to attract both winged and non-winged visitors.

The wooded trail splits near its end, one trail exiting at Jibstay Court and the other at Binnicle Way. Stumbling out of the forest onto these house-lined streets startles, an instant reminder of the world forgotten for a time.

After walking back to the gazebo, the path straight ahead provides perhaps the best view of the freshwater swale. This is a remnant of a wetland habitat that once stretched across much of the island's length.

The trail meanders through grassy areas of the preserve before heading back to the parking lot. But before heading out, cross the roadway to view residents of the adjacent pond.

Lafitte's Cove Nature Preserve is a unique gem among this West Bay subdivision. And setting aside a bit of nature is always a good thing, whether voluntary or required.

—*"Saving room for nature: Lafitte's Cove Nature Preserve is a gem" published July 9, 2014*

∧ *A paved trail runs through the nature preserve.*

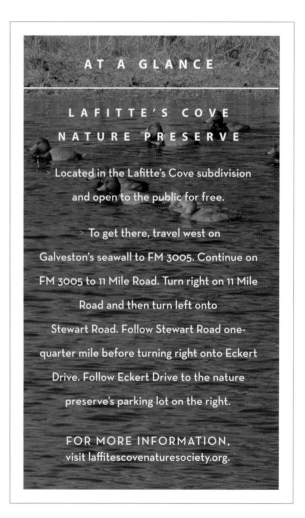

AT A GLANCE

LAFITTE'S COVE NATURE PRESERVE

> Located in the Lafitte's Cove subdivision and open to the public for free.

> To get there, travel west on Galveston's seawall to FM 3005. Continue on FM 3005 to 11 Mile Road. Turn right on 11 Mile Road and then turn left onto Stewart Road. Follow Stewart Road one-quarter mile before turning right onto Eckert Drive. Follow Eckert Drive to the nature preserve's parking lot on the right.

FOR MORE INFORMATION,
visit laffitescovenaturesociety.org.

Thick vegetation, including Sabal palms, salt cedar, marsh elder and sea myrtle, surrounds this section of a narrow, dry waterway.

A natural world with an unnatural beginning

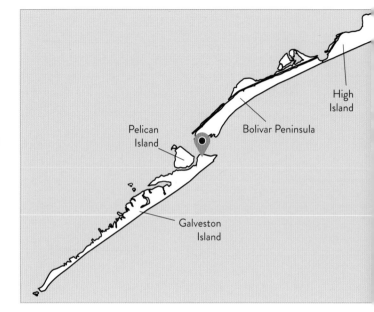

I ONLY NOTICED THE PLAQUE as I began to walk away. The faded gray background and lettering perfectly matched the elevated platform and railing.

The carved letters read "Jackson's Perch" in recognition of the U.S. Army Corps of Engineers' Richard Jackson for his "effort, support and leadership in making the Corps Woods a reality."

I don't know who Jackson was, but evidently we have him to thank for the Corps Woods Nature Sanctuary, the 10-acre thicket just off Ferry Road on Galveston Island's East End.

Perhaps he was the one who proposed using material dredged from surrounding waterways to create the land I was standing on. The Corps used to call material removed from waterways "dredge spoil" but now refers to it as "beneficial use material."

On the July morning of my visit, migratory birds didn't fill the trees but there was still much to see, starting with a dense and diverse array of plant life as soon as you pass through the gate.

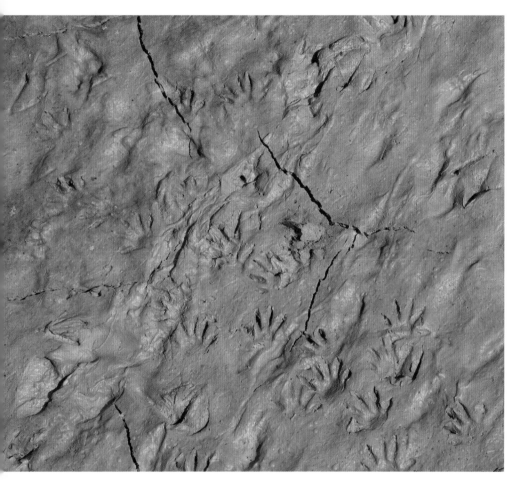

Tracks of water birds and raccoons are visible in the waterway's wet mud. ^

As I walked the gravel trail to the right, on one side grows a dense ground cover of Indian blanket, camphor daisy, southern dewberry, sea ox-eye daisy, western ragweed, sunflower and prickly pear. The other side showcases oaks, Sabal palms, hackberry trees and scattered dead limbs rising skyward, fronted in certain spots by yaupon and dense stands of an invasive plant called Brazilian pepper trees.

The gravel trail led to an elevated boardwalk that traversed a narrow waterway. Vegetation grew thickly along each bank, with invasive salt cedar, marsh elder, sea myrtle, rattle bush and a few Chinese tallow trees packed closely together.

The waterway itself was dry but only recently so, as evidenced by small frogs jumping along and wet mud imprinted with the tracks of water birds and raccoons.

Back at the entrance, I walked the gravel trail to the left, seeing much the same until I reached another elevated boardwalk traversing the same narrow waterway. Water was still present, covered in duckweed and no doubt full of a bountiful crop of small fish and frogs. Night herons, a white ibis, a snowy egret and several whistling ducks waded along the waterway, taking full advantage of the plentiful resources.

Along the trail, butterflies and bees visited flowers, dragonflies searched for mosquitoes, grasshoppers hopped about, a male cardinal flew past, spiderwebs draped across tree branches and a bird's nest clung to high branches of a tree.

I left with a sense that I had experienced a piece of our natural world. Who could possibly guess that this place had its origin as dredged material?

—*"Natural world, unnatural beginning: Sanctuary began from dredge spoil" published August 13, 2014*

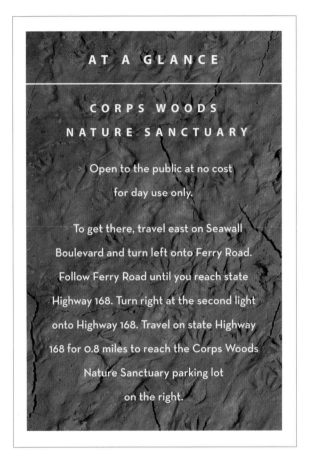

AT A GLANCE

CORPS WOODS NATURE SANCTUARY

> Open to the public at no cost for day use only.

To get there, travel east on Seawall Boulevard and turn left onto Ferry Road. Follow Ferry Road until you reach state Highway 168. Turn right at the second light onto Highway 168. Travel on state Highway 168 for 0.8 miles to reach the Corps Woods Nature Sanctuary parking lot on the right.

< The sea nettle is one of the featured jellyfish in the "Jellies" exhibit at Moody Gardens' Aquarium Pyramid.

Top
Attractions

Chapter 4

< *A sand tiger shark shows its rows of razor-sharp teeth in the Caribbean exhibit.*

The world below the water's surface

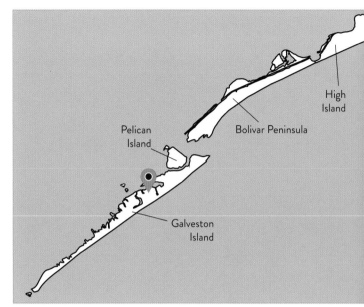

A HUNDRED FEET AWAY, I caught sight of a 10-foot shark. With a cone-shaped snout and razor-sharp teeth, I knew it was a sand tiger, a dangerous shark worth keeping an eye on. It swam toward me and within seconds was directly overhead, within arm's reach.

I didn't panic. I actually wasn't worried at all. But it wasn't bravery. It was the thick glass separating the shark in the water from me in the tunnel beneath the Caribbean exhibit at Moody Gardens' Aquarium Pyramid.

The Caribbean exhibit is the largest and perhaps favorite exhibit at the aquarium. Let's just say these aren't your average fish. It is home to large denizens like sharks, stingrays, barracuda, jack crevalle, yellowtail snapper and snook.

But it's the seals and sea lions of the North Pacific exhibit that are the first sea creatures you'll meet when entering the aquarium. Accomplished swimmers, they never seem to tire of ceaseless water acrobatics. So forget about taking a good still photograph. Just watch and be entertained.

Riley and Squirt are two of the exhibit's permanent residents. Riley, a harbor seal, was born at the Moody Gardens aquarium, while Squirt is a rehabilitated California sea lion that cannot be released because of blindness.

Then there are the wall-lined exhibits devoted to sea horses. As I watched one tank, manna from heaven in the form of live brine shrimp dropped into the water. The hungry sea horses instantly released their tail grips and excitedly swam about sucking this gift into their long snouts.

You might even spot a pregnant male sea horse. That's right, an oddity of the animal world: The male sea horse sports a brood pouch within which the female deposits eggs. He fertilizes the eggs and carries them until giving birth, contractions and all, to miniature sea horses about a half-inch long.

Another favorite are the penguins of the South Atlantic exhibit. Four species — King, Chinstrap, Rockhopper and Gentoo — live in an exhibit that resembles the rocky beaches of the sub-Antarctic

∧ *King, Chinstrap and Gentoo penguins live in the cold-climate South Atlantic exhibit.*

islands. Like their home far south, their Texas home is kept cold, at a temperature a few degrees above freezing. To keep them warm, they sport a thick layer of fat, or blubber, and overlapping, densely packed feathers.

In the South Pacific exhibit, the colorful fish offer a sampling of the color and beauty that are the norm for coral reefs. The clown triggerfish, for instance, has a bright yellow mouth encircled by a ring of white. The eyestripe surgeonfish has a bright blue tail fin and jagged blue lines along its yellowish body. And the foxface is hard to miss with its bright yellow body and black-and-white striped face.

Although the fish are the main attraction, the coral polyps are the most critical members of this tropical world. They are the tiny organisms that construct the massive structures we know as coral reefs. But they take their time, depositing their limestone exoskeleton ever so slowly, in many cases at a rate of less than 1 inch per year.

∧ *A close-up view of live coral polyps, the master builders of coral reefs.*

Coral polyps can only do their work under a rigid set of environmental conditions. They require light and clear, warm, salty water. You may have heard that the world's coral reefs are in trouble. This is why. As these necessary conditions slowly disappear in our oceans, reefs are declining.

And of course, there are the sea turtles. Five species live in the Gulf of Mexico and you can find four of them here: hawksbill, green, loggerhead and Kemp's ridley. All four are either threatened or endangered species.

Sure, there are no leaping dolphins or killer whales, the megastars of the aquarium world. But you will find the rest of the ocean's superstars.

—*"Seeing under sea: A biologist tours Moody Gardens Aquarium" published September 26, 2012*

AT A GLANCE

AQUARIUM PYRAMID AT MOODY GARDENS

> Located at One Hope Boulevard.

> New exhibits, including a Gulf of Mexico oil rig exhibit and a new penguin habitat, opened in May 2017 as part of a $37 million renovation.

FOR MORE INFORMATION,

visit moodygardens.com or call

800-582-4673.

< Cotton-top tamarin, a popular rain forest resident, are often seen along the walkway.

A rain forest on the Texas coast

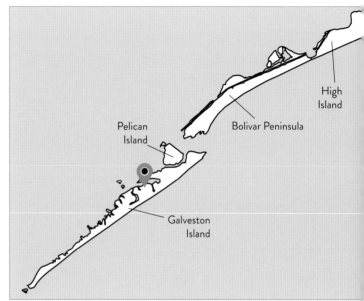

RAIN FORESTS are hot and wet. The sun beats down for 12 hours a day, and rainfall averages at least 160 inches each year. Not exactly the climate you'd expect to find on the Texas coast. But you won't have to travel to the Amazon to explore this unique forest. Inside a glass pyramid at Moody Gardens, the perfect mix of light, warmth and moisture supports an assemblage of 1,000 plants and animals moved from rain forests around the world.

The Rainforest Pyramid has been a fixture at Moody Gardens since the early 1990s, but the $25 million renovation following Hurricane Ike has remade it into a jewel.

The renovated exhibit, opened in 2011, takes visitors to a whole new level, literally. Upon entering, visitors climb stairs and pass through glass doors to a warm, humid tropical paradise surrounded by tree and palm leaves. The elevated 300-foot walkway, called the Tree Top Trail, offers a birds-eye view of the rain forest.

A canopy of six enormous ficus trees, some reaching halfway up the 10-story pyramid, envelops the walkway. Cascades of 30-foot fibrous roots dangle from their limbs, while an arsenal of aerial roots arise from their trunks, penetrating soil and grabbing rock.

^ *Colorful butterflies are attracted to the sweetness of oranges.*

These trees are some of the few survivors of Hurricane Ike's saltwater surge that flooded the rain forest floor in 2008. Unlike many of the other tropical plants and animals that perished in a salty brew, these ficus trees survived and now provide much of the green canvas for the new exhibit.

From the walkway, you can spot white-faced Saki monkeys, cotton-top tamarins and two-toed sloths — those hairy tree lovers who spend a lot of time hanging upside down from limbs.

There are exotic birds and butterflies, deadly snakes, poison dart frogs and big-eyed fruit bats that enjoy munching on fruits and nectar from flowers.

Then there are rain forest residents most likely to be heard before seen. The colorful — and loud — macaws stand guard on perches above the freshwater fish exhibit.

But some of the world's most dreaded animal species also call the rain forest home. The green anaconda is the world's heaviest snake, weighing as much as 550 pounds. It delights in squeezing its prey to death.

Tiny in comparison, but just as fearsome, are the red-bellied piranhas. With powerful jaws and razor-sharp teeth, they can clean flesh from bone within seconds.

There's an emperor scorpion, a large black-colored beauty with a venom-filled tail barb. And vampire bats hang upside down, digesting their diet of fresh animal blood.

Amidst the animal activity are hundreds of tropical plants — colorful pink orchids, bromeliads, carnivorous pitcher plants, palms, bamboo, spider plants, African violets, bird of paradise and plants that are sources of products we consume every day, like coffee, chocolate, cinnamon, vanilla and bananas.

One exhibit, however, left me wondering. At the leafcutter ants display, the sign says these little creatures cut leaves into pieces they use to cultivate fungi, the principal part of their diet.

∧ *Macaws survey their surroundings at the Amazon River fish exhibit.*

< Rain forests support a wide array of tropical plants, including colorful orchids.

But the exhibit was empty. Had they escaped into their own little heaven, a world of leaves?

This recreated rain forest delivers a simple conservation message: Rain forests support a vast array of plants, many useful to man, and animals found nowhere else. But even so, these unique ecosystems are in danger, being lost at an alarming rate to deforestation.

Near the exit, the take-home message reads: "We need to save this precious living laboratory for ourselves and for future generations."

—*"Unique ecosystems: A biologist explores island's*
$25 million renovated Rainforest"
published November 30, 2011

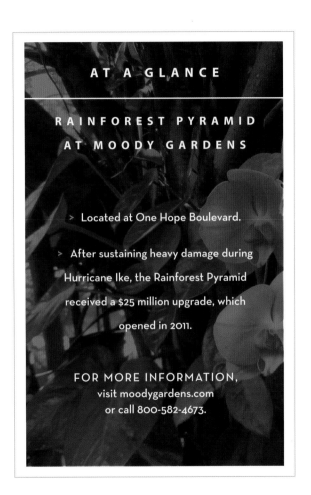

AT A GLANCE

RAINFOREST PYRAMID
AT MOODY GARDENS

> Located at One Hope Boulevard.

> After sustaining heavy damage during Hurricane Ike, the Rainforest Pyramid received a $25 million upgrade, which opened in 2011.

FOR MORE INFORMATION,
visit moodygardens.com
or call 800-582-4673.

< The Ocean Star Offshore Drilling Rig and Museum is open for tours.

Nautical charms along the island's harbor

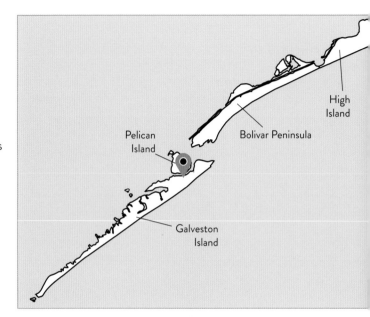

THE STRAND is one of the most popular places to shop on Galveston Island. But I've often wondered how many of the tens of thousands of visitors who walk the street each year realize the treasures awaiting just past the shops.

Galveston's harbor front is only a few blocks away. Allow me to lead the way.

To reach the harbor, walk eastward along The Strand, take a left at 20th Street and continue across Harborside Drive to the harbor.

After arriving at the waterfront, stand near the walkway to the Ocean Star Offshore Drilling Rig and Museum and look to the right. This is Pier 19, listed in the U.S. National Register of Historic Places. It has served as the berth of Galveston's historic Mosquito Fleet — the island's commercial shrimp flotilla — for more than 150 years.

At times, the shrimp boats are at rest. The captains and crews are gone, nets and doors are hoisted high in the air, and the birdlike wings are folded upward to the sky.

But when shrimp season arrives, captains and crews reappear. Nets will open and wings will spread in hopes of capturing the bounty of the sea.

Galveston's commercial shrimp fleet at rest at Pier 19. ∧

Stroll down the boardwalk to get a close-up view of the fleet in their berths. You'll notice no two boats are alike. Each has its own character, size, shape, colors and rigging, with fanciful names printed on the sides — names like Rock Bottom and Shirley B. Shrimpin.

Along the waterfront, concrete breakwater and wooden pilings are coated in white — not paint, but a gift from the birds. You might notice it on the boardwalk, railings and even on the shrimp boats. You might even smell it in the air.

The prevalence of guano is because of the congregating birds, including brown pelicans, white pelicans in winter, cormorants and laughing gulls. Close-up views are common.

After taking in the sights of shrimp boats and birds along the boardwalk, look across the slip to the back of the two fish houses that sell a variety of seafood.

Fishing boats offload their catch there and workers throw fish scraps into the water, where brown pelicans happily accept the hand-out. Other pelicans wander around the back entryway, a fact of life in a fish house.

Across the slip at the far end is where charter and party boats dock. These offer deep sea and bay fishing. The boats leave early in the morning and return late in the day, often with railings loaded with red snapper, spadefish, kingfish and Spanish mackerel.

Once dockside, most fishermen hand over their catch to men with filet knives. These men quickly practice their craft, returning thick filets while discarding spent carcasses into the water.

While standing near the far end of the boardwalk, glance next door to Pier 18. This is the Del Monte dock, where occasionally one can watch the offloading of fresh fruit, mainly bananas. During Hurricane Ike, rising waters lifted some of their trucks and deposited them into the Pier 19 slip.

After walking back along the boardwalk, move northward to the long wharf that fronts the Galveston Ship Channel.

Straight across the channel is a view of the Pelican Island shipyards, where drilling rigs are refitted and ships are dry-docked for cleaning and repair.

∧ *Across the channel is the busy shoreline of the Pelican Island shipyards.*

*The Carnival Liberty cruise ship awaits departure ∧
as the Seagull II offloads passengers.*

To the right is a view toward Bolivar Roads, the entry from the Gulf of Mexico to Galveston Bay. To the left is a view of the causeway that leads to Pelican Island. The scene sometimes even includes a cruise ship.

Walk westward to the end of the wharf to the Texas Seaport Museum, located at Pier 22. Docked here is the Seagull II, a boat that offers a tour of the harbor, often complete with encounters of bottlenose dolphins.

Towering over the museum buildings are the masts and rigging of the 1877 Tall Ship Elissa.

This short walking tour from Piers 19 to 22 will give you a view of the gems of Galveston's harbor front. Along the way, I hope you make some discoveries of your own.

—*"Nautical charms: Discover treasures in a tour near The Strand" published February 6, 2011*

The 1877 Tall Ship Elissa is docked at the ^
Texas Seaport Museum.

AT A GLANCE

GALVESTON HARBOR

> Audio tours of the Elissa are offered at the Texas Seaport Museum gift shop located at Pier 22.

> Harbor tours are available aboard the Seagull II at Pier 22.

Along this stretch of the harbor is Pier 21 Theater, which shows short family-friendly documentaries about the 1900 hurricane, pirates and other local history. It is located at 21st Street and Harborside Drive on the second floor.

> Fresh seafood markets operate at Pier 19 and various seafood restaurants line the harborfront.

FOR MORE INFORMATION,
visit galvestonhistory.org or call 409-765-3435.

< *Oyster reefs and salt marshes dominate this Galveston Bay inlet northeast of Point Bolivar Lighthouse.*

Charms of Bolivar Peninsula

Chapter 5

< *Once adorned in black-and-white horizontal bands, Point Bolivar Lighthouse is now a rust-colored brown.*

A timeless beacon still standing

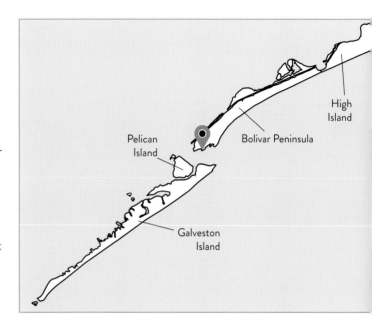

DURING THE AGE of sailing ships, entering shallow coastal waters could be a frightful and sometimes disastrous experience. Imagine being aboard a 19th-century sailing ship in these conditions as it nears a bay entrance headed for port.

It's a stormy, moonless night. A fierce wind is blowing and stirring the waters. You see nothing in the darkness that surrounds you, not a single landmark to guide your path. Anxiety grows as your eyes search the shore for a sign of land, any sign to give you a position and a safe bearing.

Now imagine the thankfulness for a sign that helped guide the way.

The beacon of a lighthouse blinks at you, providing that sign you desperately searched for. What a relief! What a joy! Now you know your position and in which direction to head toward safe harbor.

Lighthouses were built to safely guide ships through shallow coastal waters before the modern age of power and navigation. Hundreds of lighthouses dot the nation's coastlines. Galveston's lighthouse, the Point Bolivar Lighthouse, guided thousands of ships safely through the confines of Bolivar Roads.

Built in 1872, Point Bolivar Lighthouse stood 117 feet tall. She was made of bricks covered by riveted iron plates. At the top of the tower, the equipment consisted of a kerosene lamp and Fresnel lens capable of casting light seaward for up to 17 miles.

After 61 years, her time of mariner service ended in 1933 when she gave way to the South Jetty light and other modern navigational aids.

Photographed in 1917, Point Bolivar Lighthouse guided ships for 61 years. ^
(Courtesy of National Archives and Records Administration)

Point Bolivar Lighthouse's Fresnel lens, similar to the one shown here, was removed after decommissioning and is now on display at the Smithsonian's National Museum of American History in Washington, D.C. >

But during her decades of mariner service were two episodes of humanitarian service. During the hurricane of 1900, the lighthouse sheltered more than 120 people upon her 137-step spiral staircase, and up to 60 residents sought refuge there during the 1915 hurricane.

During both hurricanes, people safely huddled as the storm surge battered the lighthouse base and winds in excess of 120 mph shook and swayed the tower.

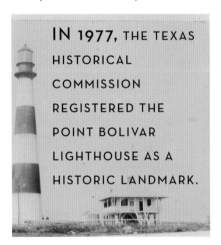

IN 1977, THE TEXAS HISTORICAL COMMISSION REGISTERED THE POINT BOLIVAR LIGHTHOUSE AS A HISTORIC LANDMARK.

In 1947, the U.S. government sold the lighthouse as surplus property to a private owner. Today, it remains in private hands and is not open to the public.

But in the late 1960s, the lighthouse and grounds were opened to a film crew for the television movie *My Sweet Charlie* starring Patty Duke and Al Freeman Jr. Its characters, a pregnant white Southern teenager and a falsely accused black New York lawyer, meet in an old abandoned lighthouse.

In 1977, the Texas Historical Commission registered the Point Bolivar Lighthouse as a historic landmark.

Today, the lighthouse still sits on the ground it has shaded for nearly 150 years. Her lamp and lens are gone, removed after her long years of service. Her iron plates have rusted to a deep dark brown. Hurricanes continue to batter her base and sway her tower. And the rising waters of Galveston Bay creep closer to her neighbor, Highway 87.

Despite being rusty and perhaps neglected, many people still stop and take a picture. Many more turn their head and gaze upward at her tower as they pass.

Although she has outlived her usefulness, and despite her age and wear, Point Bolivar Lighthouse continues to fascinate. She still holds a timeless beauty that must be captured, that must be seen.

—"Timeless beacon shines on Bolivar"
published June 2010

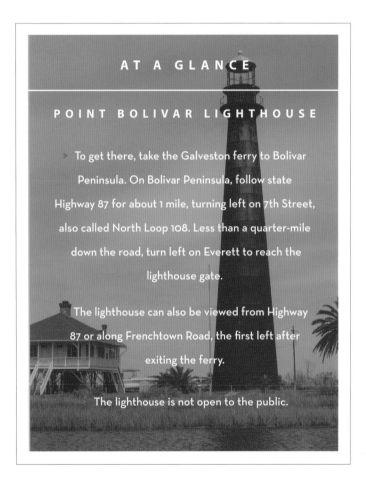

AT A GLANCE

POINT BOLIVAR LIGHTHOUSE

> To get there, take the Galveston ferry to Bolivar Peninsula. On Bolivar Peninsula, follow state Highway 87 for about 1 mile, turning left on 7th Street, also called North Loop 108. Less than a quarter-mile down the road, turn left on Everett to reach the lighthouse gate.

The lighthouse can also be viewed from Highway 87 or along Frenchtown Road, the first left after exiting the ferry.

The lighthouse is not open to the public.

< Bolivar's North Jetty is a 5-mile-long wall of rocks that traps sand flowing westerly in longshore currents. A walkway extends a quarter-mile along the jetty.

A bird magnet

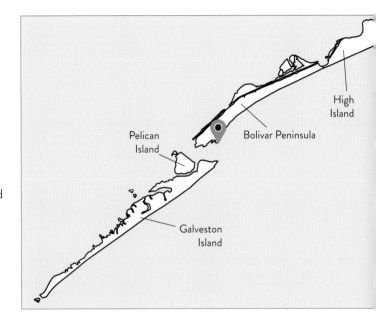

CONSTRUCTION OF Bolivar's North Jetty, completed in 1898, changed everything along that stretch of the Texas coast.

This wall of rocks, stretching 5 miles out to sea, blocked the movement of westerly flowing longshore currents. Thwarted currents thus changed course, turning shoreward and as a result began dumping their loads of sand along the east side of the North Jetty.

As this rerouting of sand-carrying currents deprived Galveston beaches of sand, it proved to be a bonanza for Bolivar Peninsula. Sand accumulation over 100 years transformed the area into a world-class birding destination called Bolivar Flats Shorebird Sanctuary.

For more than a century, longshore currents carried in and deposited untold tons of sediment, forming beachfront dune ridges that provided enough protection for the development of mud flats behind them.

Flats formed and grew, fed and nourished daily by tides. Despite being located on the beach side of the peninsula, this area today closely resembles an estuarine salt marsh, with its wide-open mud flats bordered by oysters and a broad, dense band of cordgrass, all fed daily by tidal waters flowing through inlets and meandering creeks. And like salt marshes, this area is very productive.

126

A bird-filled Bolivar Flats is a common sight in the spring. ^

Tidal waters bring in a diet of nutrients that feed cordgrasses and a variety of other plant producers such as algae, seagrasses and phytoplankton.

Nutrient pulses, aided by the warmth and radiance of sunshine, produce a cornucopia of plant matter that supports a food chain leading to a bountiful crop of amphipods, worms, clams, snails, shrimp, crabs and small fish. It is this bounty that attracts the 37 species of birds that come here by the hundreds of thousands each year.

Upon arrival, each has its own strategy for harvesting their fair share of food. Some, such as pelicans and terns, perform kamikaze dives for fish. Others, like herons and egrets, wade through the water in search of fish, shrimp and crabs. Avocets and spoonbills use a different strategy:

swishing their bill back and forth through the water and mud to latch on to whatever they can find. Still others, such as sandpipers, dunlins, dowitchers and godwits, probe the mud with pointed bills seeking a rich buried invertebrate treasure.

IT IS THIS BOUNTY THAT ATTRACTS THE 37 SPECIES OF BIRDS THAT COME HERE BY THE HUNDREDS OF THOUSANDS EACH YEAR.

The seemingly endless supply of food is one reason this place is referred to as the "crown jewel" of birding sites along the upper Texas Coast.

But the best time of year to visit Bolivar Flats may be early spring. That's when you'll find a mix of year-round birds, including herons, egrets, gulls, terns, willets, sanderlings and brown pelicans, and overwintering birds, including white pelicans, American avocets, western sandpipers, dunlins, dowitchers and godwits.

But no matter when you go, you can count on an experience unlike anything else our coastal area has to offer.

—*"Bolivar Flats: A bird magnet" published April 19, 2014*

AT A GLANCE

BOLIVAR FLATS SHOREBIRD SANCTUARY

> To get there, take the Galveston ferry to Bolivar Peninsula. On Bolivar Peninsula, follow state Highway 87 for about 2 miles, turning right on 17th Street. Follow 17th Street to its end at the North Jetty. The jetty provides a great vantage point to view birds using the extensive mud flats.

> For a view of birds on the beachfront, return to state Highway 87, turning right and traveling about 2 miles to Rettilon Road. Turn right on Rettilon Road, and follow it to the beach. On the beach, turn right and travel down the beach a short distance, parking at the vehicular barricade.

The 5-mile-long North Jetty includes a quarter-mile walkway.

FOR MORE INFORMATION, visit houstonaudubon.org/sanctuaries/bolivar-flats or call 713-932-1639.

< Silver flashes on the water's surface in the distance, likely the result of fish trying to escape predators, attract a group of brown pelicans.

Miles and miles of shoreline

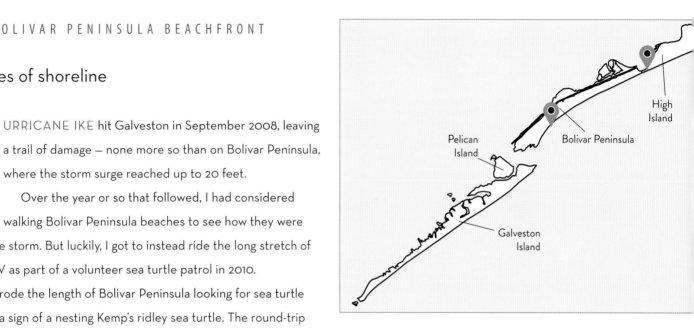

Pelican Island

Bolivar Peninsula

High Island

Galveston Island

HURRICANE IKE hit Galveston in September 2008, leaving a trail of damage — none more so than on Bolivar Peninsula, where the storm surge reached up to 20 feet.

Over the year or so that followed, I had considered walking Bolivar Peninsula beaches to see how they were recovering after the storm. But luckily, I got to instead ride the long stretch of coastline on an ATV as part of a volunteer sea turtle patrol in 2010.

Once a week, I rode the length of Bolivar Peninsula looking for sea turtle tracks in the sand, a sign of a nesting Kemp's ridley sea turtle. The round-trip route took six to seven hours and covered about 50 miles.

I rode this route 13 times from April 1 to July 15, covering a total distance of 650 miles. I never saw a turtle and spotted only one set of tracks. But what I did see that spring and early summer was an equally welcome sight.

One early June morning, when the Gulf was unusually calm, I noticed a sprinkling of silver flashes on the water's surface near shore. The flashes appeared mile after mile.

I quickly realized each flash was a fish breaking through the surface in a desperate attempt to escape a predator, most likely a large speckled trout.

As I traveled just above the water's edge, I saw all the refuse, carcasses and flotsam cast up by the gulf — ropes, fishing gear, hard hats, plastic bags, bottles and other odds and ends. I saw the expected rafts of seaweed and jellyfish, but I was startled to find two dead bottlenose dolphins, seven dead Kemp's ridley sea turtles and dozens of dead migratory birds.

In early July, the heavy rains spawned by Hurricane Alex washed rafts of a floating plant called water hyacinth out of bayous, into bays and eventually onto Bolivar beaches. Water hyacinth on local beaches is not unusual, but this water hyacinth was coated in oil.

The oil was from the Deepwater Horizon spill off Louisiana's coast. So, oil from that spill did reach local waters and beaches, but thankfully very little.

Although oil from Louisiana's Deepwater Horizon spill ∧ didn't heavily soil Texas beaches, isolated patches did find their way to Bolivar Peninsula.

I saw not only what had been cast ashore by the waves, but what had voluntarily ventured onto the beach from inland, including an American alligator and a diamondback terrapin turtle. Both were seemingly in good health.

Perhaps they were just wandering, as I do occasionally. The alligator proved friendly, because when I stopped, he walked toward me and sat down in the shade of the ATV.

There he remained until a wildlife official came to move him elsewhere. The terrapin displayed a single-minded purpose — to escape. But I was eventually able to move him to a local salt marsh, his usual habitat.

After Hurricane Ike, there was a tremendous effort to put sand back on Bolivar beaches. Although visitors can enjoy many areas of wide beach, there still are sections where the highway is alarmingly close, especially east of Rollover Pass.

The worst area is near High Island, where gulf waters wash the shore within 100 feet of the road, making it prone to flooding during high tide events.

The dunes on the peninsula benefited from the repair work of both man and nature. Nature moves slowly, but its work was already evident in the dune plants that repopulated the upper shores and now trap sand at their bases. Man-made walls of sand were constructed and planted with the common dune plant called beach panic.

On every trip, my ride was accompanied by the chorus of pile drivers and hammers, as homes were being rebuilt. As I passed remnants of homes claimed by Ike or other hurricanes, I couldn't help but wonder at the wisdom of putting another generation of houses in harm's way.

But homes weren't the only sights reemerging. East of Rollover Pass, I often passed flocks of terns and flocks of a hundred or more brown pelicans resting on the shore. Everywhere, laughing gulls filled the sky.

The fish, walkers, fishermen and beachgoers had also returned. Bolivar's beaches were back.

—"Comeback is remarkable for beaches on Bolivar"
published August 25, 2010

∧ *Nature rebuilds dunes by slowly trapping wind-blown sand at the base of repopulated plants.*

< A view of the Claybottom Pond Rookery, full of nesting birds.

A birding paradise

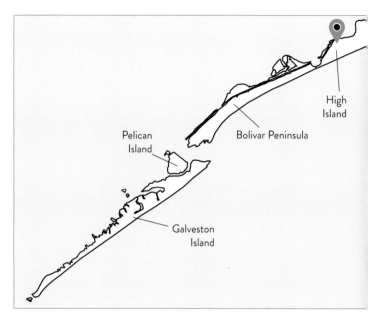

THE DAY DIDN'T START WELL. I saw only two birds at my first stop. And the dark clouds overhead threatened rain at any moment.

But it never rained and I left with a birding experience I'll never forget.

My day started at Boy Scout Woods, one of four Houston Audubon Society's bird sanctuaries on High Island.

Their open house on the day of my visit attracted a big crowd, perhaps the reason I saw only two birds on my mid-day walk through the woods. They were two crested caracaras flying in the distance as I stood on the wetland observation platform.

By early afternoon, I headed to Smith Oaks, the largest of High Island's four sanctuaries. I parked at the Old Mexico Road entrance and headed down the trail toward Claybottom Pond. I joined a half-dozen others on an observation platform overlooking the pond.

The steady drone I heard to my left came from the birds of the rookery, a portion of which I could see through the willows. Above the drone, I heard the unmistakable drumming calls of two male bullfrogs — first one, then the other, over and over, both intent on outcompeting the other for a mate.

Neotropic cormorants, great egrets and roseate spoonbills ∧
fill willow trees on Heron Island.

On a nearby shoreline, I spotted an American bittern, motionless, eyes peering into shallow water. I glanced away for a moment to watch coots picking at water plants, and when I looked back, the bittern was gulping down a fish.

As I stood still and watched, cormorants and great egrets flew by with regularity, one after the other. Soon, their mission became clear. Each flew back to the rookery with a nest-building twig in tow.

I then moved on to the next platform, one built directly next to the bird rookery on Heron Island, a U-shaped island. This vantage point offers a close-up, unobstructed view of the Claybottom Pond Rookery.

Willow trees lined the edges of the island and it seemed as if every branch of every tree hung heavy with birds. At the top were Neotropic cormorants, with great egrets and roseate spoonbills filling in the spaces below.

The breeding colors of the great egrets and roseate spoonbills were vivid at such a close range. Striking was the lime green around the eyes of the great egrets and the orange tails and orange-lined eyes of the roseate spoonbills.

The birds were mostly busy. Some were already nesting, while others built nests one twig at a time. Still others, like great egrets, were spreading their elegant, long white plumes in an attempt to attract a mate.

As I watched, I couldn't help but hear a trio best described as croaks, gurgles and oinks. But being unfamiliar with bird voices, their source and meaning remain a mystery.

I moved to an area with a view of the open side of Heron Island. Here, I counted six large alligators on the banks and in the water, their presence indicating some degree of success in harvesting from this massive collection of breeding birds and offspring.

In the pamphlet "Birds of the Rookery," the Houston Audubon Society states: "No other place in Texas allows for such an intimate view of the home life of colonial water birds."

Sounds like good old Texas bragging. But it's not bragging if it's true.

—*"Intimate view: High Island's rookery a must-see for birders" published May 7, 2014*

AT A GLANCE

BIRD SANCTUARIES ON HIGH ISLAND

To get there, take the ferry from Galveston to Bolivar Peninsula and follow state Highway 87 to where it ends at High Island. Turn left onto state Highway 124 and follow it up the hill a short distance into High Island, turning right onto Seventh Street. Turn left on Weeks Avenue and right onto Old Mexico Road. Watch for the Smith Oaks Sanctuary sign on the left. Turn left and travel to the parking lot. After parking, follow the trail to the right to reach the rookery.

Day passes and one-year passes are available.

FOR MORE INFORMATION, visit houstonaudubon.org/sanctuaries/high-island or call 713-932-1639.

< The iconic Murdochs souvenir shop on the seawall, seen here after Hurricane Ike in 2008, embodies Galveston's spirit of resiliency. It has since been rebuilt for the fourth time since the 1900 Storm.

COASTAL ECOSYSTEMS are influenced not only by normal conditions that prevail from day to day, but also by occasional extraordinary events. Along the Texas coast, hurricanes and oil spills are examples of the latter. This chapter reveals how these sporadic events have impacted the coastline — both its natural systems and man-made structures. But as this book confirms, the island's beaches, marshes, parks, preserves and attractions always come back. You might even marvel at Galveston's natural and man-made wonders a little more after learning what they've overcome.

Perils from the Sea

Chapter 6

Sand loss caused the foundation to buckle under this beachfront home.

What Hurricane Ike left behind

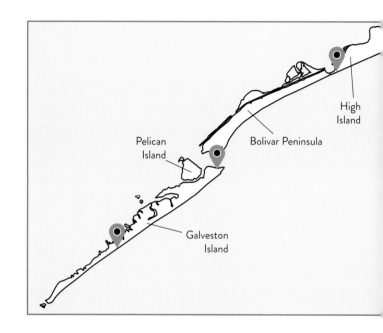

SUNSHINE SPARKLED off the calm waters of the Gulf of Mexico during my drive along Seawall Boulevard in October 2008.

I looked at what Hurricane Ike had left behind.

It made landfall Sept. 13, 2008, on the eastern end of Galveston with sustained winds of 110 mph, according to the National Weather Service.

Over a period from mid-October to mid-January, I viewed the entire beachfront, from Surfside Beach just south of Galveston up to High Island on the eastern tip of Bolivar Peninsula — a distance of 75 miles.

Sand loss at Surfside Beach caused some beachfront homes to tilt or lean at odd angles on their pilings. In some cases, houses collapsed.

*Storm surge and waves ripped apart a section of the Bluewater ∧
Highway between Surfside and San Luis Pass.*

Along Bluewater Highway between Surfside Beach and San Luis Pass, many pieces of the roadway were missing. One entire section several miles long was entirely gone, forcing me to drive along the sand.

When I reached Galveston, houses seaward of Highway 3005 that had once enjoyed a wide swath of sandy shore were now literally on the edge of the Gulf of Mexico.

At Galveston Island State Park, the beach side was virtually gone. The more than 300 feet of sand that extended south of Park Headquarters had been reduced to only a few feet.

On the eastern end of the island, Big Reef Park along Boddecker Drive had the largest amount of debris of all the places I visited. Every bit of shore was covered by debris several feet high — stairs, swings, lawn chairs, trash containers, TVs, DVDs, computer monitors and more. I also came across carcasses of a horse, two cows and a pig.

Bolivar Peninsula was the only place I could think of that might have contributed this combination of household and animal remains. And it was the only place left to look.

My wife, Pam, and I caught the ferry to Bolivar Peninsula in mid-January. Pam drove and I looked. I saw much of what I had seen before: empty and broken pilings, collapsed houses, eroded beaches and dunes, and sand moved north into pastures and roadways.

At Rollover Pass, we parked on the beach side and immediately noticed what became known as "the last house standing." There it was, intact, sitting all by itself with no other structures in sight.

∧ *Extensive sand loss put these beachfront homes at the water's edge.*

< *Mounds of debris litter the beach at Galveston Island State Park.*

< *Lumber and household items line the shore of Big Reef Park on Galveston's East End.*

We walked over to the bay side and looked out over the debris-littered mud-flat in the distance. The trailers and motor homes I remembered from previous visits were all gone, except for a few overturned, their wheels and chassis pointing skyward.

I walked eastward, past the overturned vehicles and saw only empty pilings and the eerie remnants of people's lives.

I walked a bit more eastward and then down an empty street toward the bay. While walking back, I looked eastward once more at the barren landscape that once was the town of Gilchrist.

It was then I remembered her. I read about her in the newspaper. She had lived only a few blocks away. Initially, she had decided to stay. When she finally agreed to leave, it was too late. Several feet of water covered Highway 87, her only way out. Now trapped, she waited.

During the storm, her home was washed away by a 14-foot storm surge and 20-foot waves. Some six weeks later, her body was found by a hunter in a debris field 12 miles northwest of her home.

I lowered my head. That was the saddest moment in all my days of looking.

—"What Ike left behind"
published February 24, 2009

> *At Rollover Pass on Bolivar Peninsula, Hurricane Ike flattened every structure in sight, except for this one house.*

> *Empty pilings were a common sight at Rollover Pass and other parts of Bolivar Peninsula.*

144

< *The large amount of common reed roots exposed at the ship channel's edge indicates a rapidly eroding shoreline.*

Peeling back the shore

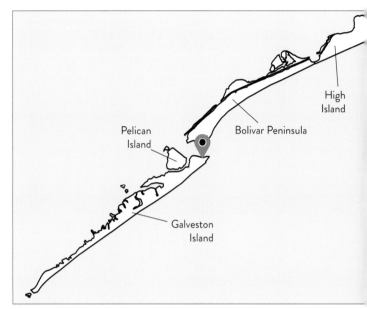

O N THE EAST END of Galveston Island is Big Reef, bordered on the south by the South Jetty and on the north by Bolivar Roads. It's one of my favorite places to visit because it mixes the sights and sounds of diverse natural habitats with the activities of a busy ship channel.

One year after Hurricane Ike hit Galveston in September 2008, I walked the 1-mile length of the Bolivar Roads shore of Big Reef, a walk I'd made many times before.

It was no longer the shoreline I remembered. Hurricane Ike's tremendous storm surge had moved through there twice. The back flow from the bay likely did most of the damage.

Before Ike, I stood just east of the beach at the edge of a tidal creek and took a photo of the wetlands. Then, the wetlands of cordgrass, mud, water and oysters were sheltered from the relentless waves of Bolivar Roads by a protective wall of sand and nourished by flood-tide seawater. I still have the photo from December 7, 2007. It was a scene of beauty, an abundance of life.

But one year after Hurricane Ike, the remains of those wetlands sat on the edge of the ship channel. Hurricane Ike's storm surge ravaged this shoreline, washing away the protective wall of sand and peeling back the shore.

In a photo taken December 7, 2007 – a year before Hurricane Ike – this ^
sheltered portion of the Big Reef shoreline consisted of a cordgrass-
dominated wetland and an abundance of oysters.

Before Ike, I walked the Big Reef shore-line eastward from the tidal creek all the way to the shore's end near the Gulf and South Jetty. Back then, there was plenty of room to meander out 100 yards or more.

After Ike, with all that sand gone, the entire Bolivar Roads shore of Big Reef had been narrowed and battered by wind-generated and ship-driven waves. The ever-present energy of rolling water was carving away at the edges of Big Reef.

Stands of common reed at the water's edge was especially alarming because this plant typically grows in fresh and brackish marsh areas, which on Big Reef are found in areas inland from the shore where rainfall accumulates. For this plant to be found directly on the shoreline, a tremendous amount of ground had been lost.

On my walk, I saw a group of cormorants resting in shallow water near the shore. As the big waves from a passing ship approached, they flew off to escape the danger but quickly returned after the waves had passed. If only the Big Reef shore could have done the same. Unfortunately, she could only sit as waves washed her side.

I don't know how Big Reef's story will end, whether nature will once again bring back the sand needed for shoreline protection and rebuilding. But for now, the evidence is clear: she is losing.

—*"Losing ground: Big Reef taking a hit more than a year after Ike"*
published October 28, 2009

∧ *This view of the same area as the opposite page photo shows the wave-battered, eroding shoreline of Big Reef one year after Hurricane Ike.*

< *Heavy machinery removes oil from Galveston's West End beaches after the 1984 Alvenus oil spill.*

Oil in the Gulf

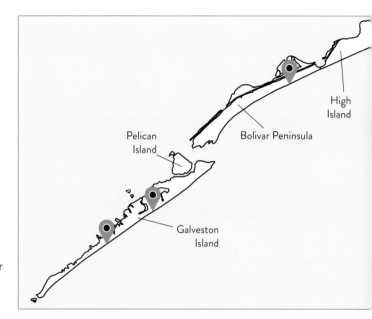

High
Island

Bolivar Peninsula

Pelican
Island

Galveston
Island

WHEN OIL IS SPILLED into the Gulf of Mexico and begins to drift toward the coastline, fears abound that it will tragically impact coastal organisms and fragile ecosystems.

Such fears arose in April 2010, after the Deepwater Horizon oil spill off the coast of Louisiana. But some 26 years earlier, another oil spill rattled Galveston Island.

In 1984, the tanker Alvenus ran aground 11 miles off the coast of Cameron, Louisiana, rupturing its hull and leaking 3 million gallons of crude oil into the Gulf of Mexico. Winds and waves moved the oil toward the Texas coastline.

At the time, I was an assistant professor at Texas A&M University at Galveston doing oil spill research, so when the spill occurred, news reporters contacted me. During my first interview, I remarked that the oil probably would disperse before reaching Galveston Island. Boy, was I wrong.

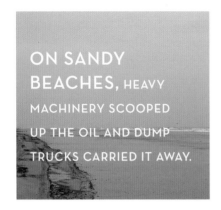

ON SANDY BEACHES, HEAVY MACHINERY SCOOPED UP THE OIL AND DUMP TRUCKS CARRIED IT AWAY.

Despite my "expert" prediction, I was asked to give my opinion on several more occasions. After the oil came ashore, I was invited to ride in a news helicopter to survey coastal impact.

Several days after the spill, heavy amounts of oil began washing ashore on Galveston and Bolivar Peninsula, and continued to cover shores for several weeks. The largest quantity of oil came ashore on the west end of the island.

Cleanup involved considerable manpower and heavy machinery. On the seawall, oil was removed from granite blocks using high-pressure spray and absorbent pom-poms and pads.

On sandy beaches, heavy machinery scooped up the oil and dump trucks carried it away.

Only small, isolated amounts of oil entered the Galveston Bay system via Rollover Pass and Bolivar Roads, so impacts to valuable wetlands and fisheries were minimal. But the oil on beaches greatly impacted tourism.

Recalling the Alvenus oil spill made me wonder how the Deepwater Horizon oil spilling into the Gulf of Mexico would impact coastal Louisiana.

I spent five years as a graduate student at Louisiana State University studying the wetlands of south Louisiana. On some days, I traveled by boat for hours and saw nothing but wetlands. On other days, with rod and reel in hand, I experienced first-hand why the area was referred to as "Sportsman's Paradise."

The wetlands present in coastal Louisiana are part of the Mississippi River Delta, a system that sits particularly exposed to such oil spills. Few blockades, such as the Gulf-side ribbons of sand like Galveston Island, exist along coastal Louisiana.

When large quantities of oil came ashore in 1984, it blanketed Galveston's West End beaches. >

High-pressure spray and absorbents were used in 1984 to clean oil from granite blocks along the western end of the seawall.

As of May 2010, it still is unclear to what extent oil will impact this marshland-rich system. My hope and that of others is the oil will be contained, cleaned, dispersed or diverted before it reaches perhaps the most ecologically important coastline in the United States.

—"Oil spill in Gulf sparks memories of 1984" published May 6, 2010

AUTHOR'S NOTE: Seven years after the 2010 Deepwater Horizon oil spill off Louisiana's coast, studies continue in an effort to determine the long-term impact on Gulf of Mexico marine animals and marshes. The spill released over 200 million gallons of oil, killing and injuring bottlenose dolphins, sea turtles, seabirds, corals and some fish. Large quantities of oil reached Louisiana's coastal marshes. Marshes lightly oiled recovered quickly, but marshes heavily oiled show signs of erosion, likely due to the death of cordgrass roots that bind marsh soil together.

Sea oats

Coastal Texas
**Plants &
Animals**

Sea purslane ∧

Here is a list of plants and animals listed by habitat that can be found on Galveston Island, Bolivar Peninsula and other areas of the Texas coast.

GULFSIDE SANDY BEACH AND DUNES

Sargassum community
Sargassum (brown algae, occasionally
washes ashore from the Gulf of Mexico)
Sargassum crab
Sargassum fish
Sargassum nudibranch
Sargassum shrimp

Plants
Amaranth
Beach evening primrose
Beach morning glory
Beach panic (bitter panicum)
Beach tea
Camphor daisy
Camphorweed
Coastal dropseed
Indian blanket
Marshhay cordgrass
Pennywort
Railroad vine
Sea oats
Sea purslane
Sea rocket
Sunflower
Water hyacinth* (occasionally washes ashore
after river runoff carries it into the Gulf of Mexico)
Western ragweed

Animals
Beach flea (amphipod)
Beach flies (tiger beetle)
Blue crab
Coquina clam (bean clam)
Ghost crab
Ghost shrimp
Hermit crab (Isocheles)
Kemp's ridley sea turtle
(females crawl ashore to nest in the dunes)
Lettered olive
Marine worm (polychaete)
Mole crab
Moon snail
Speckled crab
Tube-building worm

Birds
Brown pelican
Laughing gull
Ring-billed gull
Ruddy turnstone
Sanderling
Willet
Yellow-crowned night heron

INTERIOR FRESHWATER WETLANDS
(swales, potholes and ponds)

Plants
Black willow
Bulrush (California)
Cattail
Common reed
Deep-rooted sedge*
Duckweed
Rattle bush
Salt cedar*
Saltmarsh mallow
Saltmarsh morning glory
Spikerush
Water fern
Water hyssop
Water meal

Green treefrog
Nutria
Red-eared turtle

Birds
American bittern
American coot
Blue-winged teal
Cormorant
Great egret
Green-winged teal
Mottled duck
Northern shoveler
Pied-billed grebe
Redhead
Red-winged blackbird
Roseate spoonbill
Snowy egret
Whistling duck
White ibis

Animals
American alligator
Broad-banded water snake
Bullfrog
Dragonfly

INTERIOR COASTAL PRAIRIE AND GRASSLANDS

Plants
Bushy bluestem
Coreopsis
Dodder
Indian blanket
Little bluestem
Macartney rose
Marsh elder
Marshhay cordgrass
Prickly pear
Sea myrtle
Seaside goldenrod
Southern dewberry
Sunflower
Western ragweed
Wild indigo

Animals
Butterfly
Cottonmouth
Cotton rat
Coyote
Fire ants
Raccoon

Birds
Cardinal
Eastern meadowlark
Grackles
Kite
Mockingbird
Northern Harrier
Robin

∧ *Yellow-crowned night heron*

Saltmarsh
mallow
>

American
alligator

<

Dragonfly ⌃

Northern shoveler ⌃

INTERIOR WOODLANDS

Plants
Brazilian pepper*
Chinaberry tree*
Chinese tallow*
Dwarf palmetto
Hackberry
Live oak
Mustang grape
Sabal palm
Toothache tree
Yaupon

Animals
Cottonmouth
Cottontail rabbit
Opossum

Birds
Blue jay
Buntings (migrants)
Cardinal
Carolina wren
Mockingbird
Orioles (migrants)
Red-bellied woodpecker
Tanagers (migrants)
Vireos (migrants)
Warblers (migrants)

BAYSIDE SALT MARSH

Plants
Black mangrove
Black rush
Carolina wolfberry
Coastal dropseed
Glasswort
Gulf cordgrass
Key grass
Marshhay cordgrass
Salt cedar*
Saltgrass
Saltmarsh bulrush
Saltwort
Seablight
Sea-lavender
Sea ox-eye daisy
Smooth cordgrass

Animals
Diamond-back terrapin
Fiddler crab
Gulf salt marsh snake
Ribbed mussel
Salt marsh periwinkle

Birds
Clapper rail
Laughing gulls
Reddish egret
Red-winged blackbird
Seaside sparrow
White ibis
Willet

ADJACENT SHALLOW BAY

Seagrasses
Shoalgrass
Turtle grass
Widgeon grass

Animals
Atlantic croaker
Bay anchovy
Bay whiff
Black drum
Blue crab
Brown shrimp
Comb jellies
Flounder (southern)
Grass shrimp

Lightening whelk
Lizardfish
Longnose killifish
Menhaden
Moon jellyfish
Needlefish
Oysters (eastern)
Pinfish
Redfish
Sea nettle
Speckled trout
Spot croaker
Striped hermit crab
Striped mullet
Tidewater silverside
White shrimp

Birds
American avocet
Brown pelican
Great blue heron
Great egret
Roseate spoonbill
Snowy egret
Tricolored heron
White pelican (winter resident)

*Invasive plants of Texas Gulf coast prairies
and marshes (texasinvasives.org)

Nutria
>

Cottonmouth
>

160

BIBLIOGRAPHY

Ajilvsgi, Geyata. *Wildflowers of Texas*. Shearer Publishing, Bryan, Texas, 2003.

Anderson, John B. *The Formation and Future of the Upper Texas Coast*. Texas A&M University Press, College Station, Texas, 2007.

Andrews, Jean. *Shells and Shores of Texas*. University of Texas Press, Austin, Texas, 1977.

Antrobus, Sally E. *Galveston Bay*. Texas A&M University Press, College Station, Texas, 2005.

Basnight, Bob. *What Ship Is That? A Field Guide to Boats and Ships*. The Lyons Press, Guilford, Connecticut, 1996.

Bull, John and John Farrand Jr. *The Audubon Society Field Guide to North American Birds: Eastern Region*. Alfred A. Knopf, New York, New York, 1997.

Cannatella, Mary M. and Rita E. Arnold. *Plants of the Texas Shore: A Beachcomber's Guide*. Texas A&M University Press, College Station, Texas, 1985.

Davis, Richard A. Jr. *Beaches of the Gulf Coast*. Texas A&M University Press, College Station, Texas, 2014.

Duncan, Wilbur H. and Marion B. Duncan. *Seaside Plants of the Gulf and Atlantic Coasts*. Smithsonian Institution Press, Washington, D.C., 1987.

Edwards, Peter. *Illustrated Guide to the Seaweeds and Seagrasses in the Vicinity of Port Aransas, Texas*. University of Texas Press, Austin, Texas, 1976.

Eubanks, Ted, Robert Behrstock and Ron Weeks. *Birdlife of Houston, Galveston, and the Upper Texas Coast*. Texas A&M University Press, College Station, Texas, 2006.

Galveston Bay Estuary Program. *The Quiet Invasion: A Guide to Invasive Plants of the Galveston Bay Area*. Texas Commission on Environmental Quality. Houston, Texas, 2006.

Hoese, H. Dickson and Richard H. Moore. *Fishes of the Gulf of Mexico*. Texas A&M University Press, College Station, Texas, 1998.

Johnson, William and Mark Lockwood. *Texas Waterfowl*. Texas A&M University Press, College Station, Texas, 2013.

Jones, Leigh and Rhiannon Meyers. *Infinite Monster: Courage, Hope, and Resurrection in the Face of One of America's Largest Hurricanes*. PenlandScott Publishers, 2010.

Katz, Cathie and Paul Mikkelsen. *The Little Book of Sea-beans and other Beach Treasures*. Available from www.seabean.com, 2005.

Lehman, Roy L. *Marine Plants of the Texas Coast*. Texas A&M University Press, College Station, Texas, 2013.

Loughmiller, Campbell and Lynn Loughmiller. *Texas Wildflowers*. University of Texas Press, Austin, Texas, 2010.

Moulton, Daniel W. and John S. Jacob. *Texas Coastal Wetlands Guidebook*. Publication # TAMU-SG-00-605. Texas Sea Grant, Bryan, Texas, 2000.

Rabek, Barbara. *A Photographer's Eye: Galveston*. Blurb Creative Publishing. Available from www.lat2915.com, 2010.

Roberts, Bruce and Ray Jones. *American Lighthouses: A Definitive Guide*. The Globe Pequot Press, Guilford, Connecticut, 2002.

Rothschild, Susan B. *Beachcomber's Guide to Gulf Coast Marine Life*. Taylor Trade Publishing, Lanham, Maryland, 2004.

Spotila, James R. *Sea Turtles: A Complete Guide to Their Biology, Behavior, and Conservation*. The John Hopkins University Press, Baltimore, Maryland, 2004.

Spotila, James R. *Saving Sea Turtles: Extraordinary Stories from the Battle against Extinction*. The John Hopkins University Press, Baltimore, Maryland, 2011.

Stevenson, Jim. *Wildlife of Galveston*. VanJus Press, Galveston, Texas, 1999.

Tveten, John and Gloria Tveten. *Wildflowers of Houston and Southeast Texas*. University of Texas Press, Austin, Texas, 2010.

Weber, Michael, Richard T. Townsend and Rose Bierce. *Environmental Quality in the Gulf of Mexico: A Citizen's Guide*. Center for Marine Conservation, Washington, D.C., 1992.

INDEX